To Jim
from
John Nov. '67

LEARNING TO RIDE, HUNT and SHOW

by

GORDON WRIGHT

Completely Illustrated by

SAM SAVITT

GARDEN CITY BOOKS, GARDEN CITY, NEW YORK, 1960

A FOREWORD

by

Colonel John W. Wofford

There is an old saying to the effect that, "Those who can, do; those who can't, teach—" But every once in a while this is disproved by someone who is able to do, and at the same time translate his knowledge into a simple enough form so that even the rankest novice can understand it and follow it.

That is what Gordon Wright has done in this book.

At last, we have a simple, uncomplicated, uncluttered book that teaches riding in the same step-by-step, lesson-by-lesson method which teachers of dancing, music, languages, and some other sports have long since recognized as the only safe, sound method of teaching. Only in the field of riding has the pupil continued to have everything thrown at him at once, with the first lesson consisting of a hodge podge of everything, from learning how to mount and dismount correctly to the posting trot, to putting a horse on the proper lead for a canter.

In the years in which I have been familiar with Gordon Wright's method of teaching riding, I have seen his success with his pupils range all the way from producing young Maclay winners at the National Horse Show at Madison Square Garden in New York, to instilling confidence in people well past middle age and bringing them along to the point where they could hunt and show not only safely, but with a success which many a professional rider might envy.

Gordon Wright's own background in riding covers everything from riding and roping steers to having broken and schooled jumpers which have won in the best American horse shows for the past twenty years. During the Second World War, he was commissioned a lieutenant in the famous Cavalry School at Fort Riley, Kansas, where he went through Officer Candidate School and was later appointed to the teaching staff. Back in civilian life, he was able to combine his own practical knowledge of riding and showing with the scientific knowledge of both riding and teaching which has made the Fort Riley Cavalry School one of the finest training schools for riders and horses alike, in the world.

Gordon Wright continues as an active rider in show ring and hunt field, but his real interest lies in the *teaching* of riding, and his real genius, it seems to me, is his amazing ability to transmit his knowledge of horses and riding to the beginner in such a way that confidence is instilled, in even the most timid rider, from the very first lesson.

This unusual ability as a teacher, and his sincere interest in teaching, shows through clearly in this book. From the very first page—and the very first lesson—anyone who has ridden at all will begin to see that a great deal of the confusion, and almost all of the risk, has been taken out of learning how to ride and jump. It should serve as an invaluable handbook for the beginner and an excellent source of reference and review for the experienced rider.

John W. Wofford.

Rimrock Farm,
Milford, Kansas.

TABLE OF CONTENTS

LIST OF ILLUSTRATIONS

PREFACE

It is obviously true that no one can learn how to ride by reading a book. The purpose of this book is to help anyone who *is* learning to ride, whether he be beginner, intermediate, or advanced; whether his problem is controlling the increase and decrease of speed on the bridle path; learning the correct way to punish—and cure—a horse that is running out or refusing his fences; or mastering the coordination of the aids for the extended trot, two-tracking and flying changes of the lead.

After more than twenty-five years of teaching riding to pupils of all degrees of riding skill and ability, my basic concept of good horsemanship is that it must, first of all, be safe horsemanship. When it comes to riding, *courage* is but another word for confidence. The horse that knows that neither his back nor his mouth will be abused is the horse that gallops down to his jump with courage. The rider who knows he will not fall off, is the rider who takes his correct position coming into a jump, and holds it.

This mutual confidence is the keynote and cornerstone of all good horsemanship. It doesn't just happen. It is the result of being taught the right thing to do, and being made to do it over and over again, at the slow gaits and at the low jumps, until your reactions have become automatic.

For this reason, I have worked out a special technique of instruction to accompany each chapter in this book. Whether the pupil is fortunate enough to be able to work under the guidance of a competent instructor, or whether he is self-taught, this technique of instruction will help him rate his progress and keep him from the common fault of trying to go ahead too quickly. Once the early work has been mastered, and a secure, balanced seat in the saddle has been achieved, the pupil can move ahead very rapidly to the more advanced stages of riding.

Riders and horses alike lose their courage when they lose their confidence. They lose their confidence when they are asked to perform beyond their proven ability. In riding, the early work must never be hurried. The rider should not be put at higher fences until he asks for them. If his reactions are not entirely automatic, he should go back to the lower fences again until the rough spots are smoothed out. The horse should not be put at higher fences until he is performing quietly and smoothly over the lower fences. If he makes mistakes on the higher fences, he should return to the lower ones until that particular mistake has been overcome.

Anyone interested in learning how to ride, hunt and show will be greatly benefited by following the timetable which I have worked out in this book, and which I have used successfully with so many hundreds of pupils.

To learn how to ride, hunt and show, you *don't* have to fall off your horse three times. I consider one time more than enough! You *don't* have to be possessed of any great or special physical skills or talents. You *don't* have to be young, or thin, or tall, or short. All you have to do is be willing to learn what to do on a horse, when to do it, and have the patience to repeat the early work often enough so that your reactions become automatic.

In this book, I have explained the fundamentals of a secure, balanced seat. You will learn how to assume this correct position in the saddle, and the simple exercises which, practiced for just a few minutes of each riding hour, will soon make this position secure and automatic. The same is true of the Posting Trot, which becomes, in this book, your first simple, easy exercise toward the development of a good jumping position in the saddle. I have carefully avoided all waste motion. Each step of learning to ride with this new position, is a step toward the eventual goal of jumping and showing. The two-point and three-point contact which you will learn to use in the galloping position is the same two-point and three-point contact which you use in the approach and take-off of the jump.

The same practical, time-saving approach holds true of the rest of the material which you will find here, starting with the good and bad points of a horse's conformation which every rider should know a little about, and going on through diseases of the horse, his care, grooming, equipment and tack; the use and co-ordination of the Aids; the Five Rein Positions and their effects; Riding Hall Movements; the use of punishment and reward in training your horse; Elementary, Intermediate and Advanced jumping, and special chapters devoted to riding a course of jumps in a ring, hunter trails, show ring and hunt field etiquette and the final, advanced work involving collection, flexions, two-tracking and other special movements called for in Olympic riding.

My purpose in writing this book, like the purpose of my teaching, is to prove that safe riding, hunting and showing are within the easy reach of every rider who has the will to learn.

Gordon Wright

To the young riders of America who, in the years I have worked with them, have taught me as much about courage and good sportsmanship as I have taught them.

LEARNING TO RIDE, HUNT AND SHOW

By
Gordon Wright

PART I

THE HORSE AND HIS REGIONS

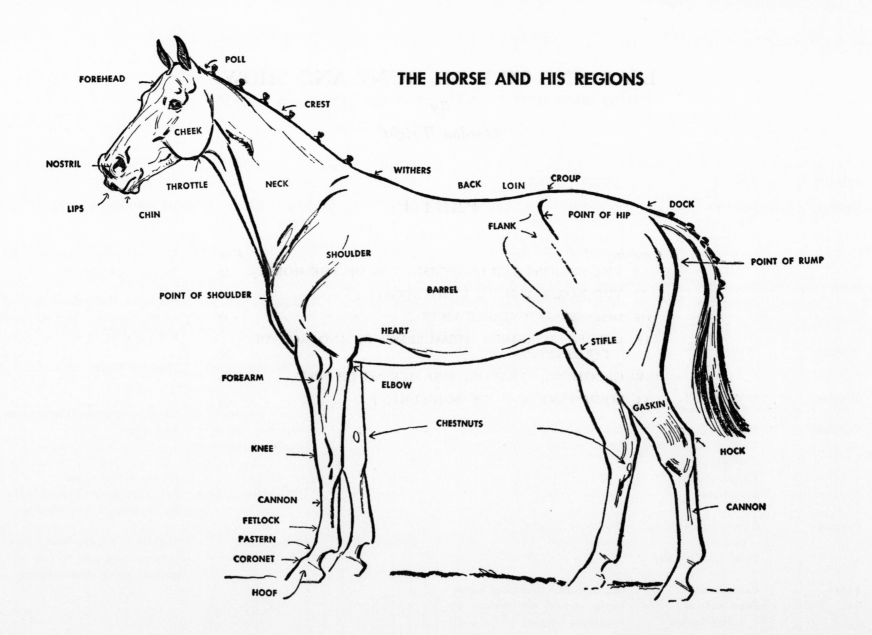

GOOD AND BAD POINTS TO LOOK FOR IN A HORSE

REGION	FAULTS	GOOD POINTS	REGION	FAULTS	GOOD POINTS
Head	Lop-ears Pig-eyed Roman-nosed Dish-faced	Small ears, set well apart Broad forehead Eyes large, set far apart Face, lean and fine	Back	Sway back Roach back	Straight, not too long
Neck	Ewe-neck Bull-necked	Long, and of a thickness consistent with the rest of the horse's body	Chest	Barrel-chested Slab-sided	Of moderate breadth, and cannot be too deep
			Loin	Long-coupled	No more than three fingers' width between last rib and point of hip
Withers	Mutton-withered	Moderately high, not too thin nor bulky with muscle	Belly	Herring-gutted or Shad-bellied	Well let down
Shoulder	Straight	Long and sloping	Croup	Goose-rumped or Rainy-day croup Hips too prominent	Good length, moderate width and slope
Cannon	Too long Tied in below knee Calf-kneed Knock-kneed Bowlegged	Short and strong Broad and flat	Hock	Cow-hocked Tied-in below hock	Clean, well defined Bones large and prominent, no roughness or puffiness
Pastern	Coon-footed (Long pastern) Short and stubby	Moderate length Correct slope	Cannon (Hind)	Sickle-hocked Curby hock	Slightly longer than front cannon; one-half to one inch greater bone measurement
Foot	Contracted Toed-out, or splay-footed Toed-in	In proportion to size of horse; heels should be broad, of moderate height			

Chapter I

GOOD AND BAD POINTS TO LOOK FOR
IN A HORSE

To be able to know and judge a horse's conformation with any degree of skill or accuracy is beyond the knowledge and ability of the average rider. When you set out to buy a horse, you should put yourself in the hands of a dealer or professional horseman, in whom you have confidence, and be guided by his advice. A great majority of bad horse deals are not the result of dishonest horse trading, but the result of the rider's having over-estimated his own riding ability so that he finds himself over-mounted; or the result of trying to purchase a single horse to fill many different needs and riding requirements.

Whether you are riding a horse that you have hired from a riding academy, or about to buy a horse of your own, the first thing to do is to get a reasonable estimate of your own riding ability. Good horses make good riders, because a good horse enables even a mediocre rider to look good; but bad riders ruin good horses. One of the surest ways to lose courage and security on a horse and start the development of bad hands, is to find yourself over-mounted. When selecting a horse which you hope to enjoy for an hour's pleasant hacking or for years of enjoyable hunting and jumping, don't over-estimate your own riding ability. Horses' habits can be changed, but their dispositions remain the same. A bold horse is always a bold horse and even cutting down on his

feed—which is my idea of one of the cruelest ways to mistreat a horse that has a day's work to do—won't make him really quiet.

If you have to err, try to err on the side of getting something that's a little less horse than you think you can safely manage. The beginner, certainly, is safer with a horse he has to urge than with one he has to hold. Until a secure seat and reasonably steady hands have been developed, it is well to be mounted on horses that do not require too much control.

The second important consideration in choosing the horse you are to ride, or to own, is deciding what you really want in a horse—a quiet hack, a horse that can hunt well and also show a little, or a horse that can be shown and jumped, but that probably will not be too well behaved in the company of the hunt field.

Every once in a while, of course, we do happen upon a combination of the horse that hunts and shows, hacks and jumps, with equal, even if not with outstanding, ability in each field. Since such a horse is the exception rather than the rule, make up your own mind what it is you want from your horse. The horse that hunts quietly and jumps well in company does not, as a rule, jump well alone, especially in the ring.

Many riding accidents would never have happened if people could control the false pride that makes them almost ashamed to ask for a quiet horse. But a good horseman can get anything he wants out of any horse, and I have never been able to figure out the illogic that makes poor riders think that they can control a high-spirited horse when, by their own admission, they can't even make the quiet horse move forward!

The good horseman is *always* mounted on a quiet horse, because whatever horse he is on seems quiet. Until you have reached the stage where your controls are able to function independently and automatically under any and all emergency conditions, always ask for a quiet horse. If you're really good enough to ride the other kind, you're good enough to get a good ride out of the "tame variety."

And when you get ready to buy a horse, have confidence in the man from whom you are buying! Go to someone who has seen you ride and knows your riding ability. Tell him frankly what your price limit is and what you expect in the way of performance. If necessary, sacrifice age to temperament, disposition and looks to jumping skill. Out of the four or five things that you want a horse to be able to do for you, if you get a horse that does one of those things really well, consider that you've made a good deal.

Meanwhile, I think you will feel better about either hiring or buying a horse for your own riding enjoyment, if you know a little bit about a horse's conformation, and how his good and bad points will affect your comfort and safety while in the saddle. Perfection is what we seek but seldom find. So remember that a good horse is one with many good points, some indifferent points, and no really bad points. Any number of good points in a horse cannot compensate for one really bad point. The body cannot be stronger than its weakest part.

Some conformation faults, while certainly not desirable, are not, on the other hand, too important. Others are important enough to render the horse either unfit or unsafe.

Another thing to bear in mind in checking your horse's good and bad points is that handsome is as handsome does. It is true that a horse cannot be too deep through the chest, as we say on the conformation chart at the beginning of this chapter. But getting a good, deep-chested horse, with plenty of room for heart and lungs to work perfectly, is no good for the rider if the heart itself isn't there. There are "chicken-hearted" horses just as there are "chicken-hearted" people. Sometimes, this is just a result of poor training and putting a horse at obstacles that are too much for him. When this is the case, it is comparatively easy to restore the horse's confidence and "nerve." But there *are* some horses who simply do not have any heart, who have to be whipped and spurred over every fence, and who take advantage of every opportunity to quit or to run out. In a jumping horse, that kind of disposition is something that would completely nullify a dozen good conformation points.

A good horse for you is a horse that is physically and temperamentally suited to your riding needs. He is a horse who can perform well, stand up under the amount of work he is going to be asked to do, and so constructed, physically, that the rider has a pleasant, enjoyable time for the hours he is in the saddle.

Some of our top conformation hunters will not measure up to those requirements, but top conformation hunters are only expected to strip well when shown in hand and to perform creditably under the artificial conditions of the show ring. They are neither asked, nor expected, to do a day's work in the hunt field, carry the timid or uncertain rider over fences, or perform smoothly and quietly enough for the young horsemanship rider to look well in horsemanship events.

After you have been scrupulously honest in your appraisal of your own—or your child's—riding ability, and decided on the kind of riding which you most enjoy—hacking, hunting, or showing—the following list of conformation faults, and the way in which they may be expected to affect your riding pleasure or your horse's staying powers, may serve as a helpful check-list.

JUG-HEAD, or HAMMER-HEAD: An overly large or jug-head on a horse is certainly a blemish, but for the average rider, that, in itself, is not too important. The important thing is that a large head acts like a heavy weight at the end of a long lever and tends to make the horse heavy in the rider's hands, to develop bad or heavy hands. Because such a horse is always hanging in the rider's hands, this is a hard kind of horse for the horsemanship rider, especially, to look well on. It's also apt to be a clumsy horse, since a horse's head and neck are his balancers, and this horse is over-weighted and, therefore, out of balance.

EWE-NECK means that the horse's neck is on him upside down. A ewe-necked horse is always a star-gazer. As a rule, a star-gazer, rushing into his fences with his head stuck up in the air, is not a safe jumper. A star-gazer will also tend to develop bad hands in a rider. The tendency is for the rider to attempt to lower the horse's head carriage by lowering the hands, thereby breaking the line from the horse's mouth to the rider's elbow. And when the hands are carried high, as they must be on this type of horse, the effect for horsemanship classes, particularly, is not good. There is no way on earth to lower the carriage of a horse's head when he is ewe-necked. To attempt to do so with tight mar-tingales and other artificial aids is only to deprive the horse of the use of his head and neck to balance himself. A ewe-necked horse is, therefore, one to avoid if possible.

BULL-NECKED: A short, thick, prominently muscled neck, and a horse that is inclined to pull or bore. It is a conformation fault often found in common bred horses.

MUTTON-WITHERED: A horse that won't carry a saddle well. The saddle is always slipping on this horse, and he is pre-disposed to such unsoundnesses as fistula and sore withers.

STRAIGHT SHOULDER: A serious conformation fault, es-pecially in a hunter or jumper. A short, upright shoulder shortens the action, stiffens the gait of the forelegs, and places the rider forward where he unduly weights the forehand. Sometimes, a horse appears to have a good shoulder when viewed from the ground, but if you are in any doubt, mount him. If, when you are in the saddle, looking down, the horse seems to "fall away" in front and not have nearly as much front as he appeared to have, you may be reasonably sure he has a straight shoulder.

LONG CANNON BONE: Means that the horse is apt to pull his check ligament, which causes lameness, or to bow his tendons.

TIED IN BELOW THE KNEE: A serious weakness. This is where a horse's bone is measured, and it means his bone is weaker at one point.

CALF-KNEED: If, when viewed from the side, the line of the forearm and cannon is bent backward at the knee, the horse is said to be calf-kneed. A calf-kneed horse has rough, jolty gaits and tends to break down easily under the strain of jumping.

OVER IN THE KNEE: "Knock-kneed" and "Bow-legged" are all terms that are self-explanatory. In addition to being confor-mation faults, they are blemishes which make the horse's work harder for him because undue strain is naturally placed on a crooked or misshapen leg that is attempting to do the work of a normal leg. The horse's usefulness is, therefore, curtailed. He is more subject to breakdowns and lamenesses.

SWAY-BACK: A hollowed-out back, and one that is not only weak but becomes rapidly worse with weight carrying and age. If the topline of the back and loin is strongly arched, the horse is said to have a "roachback" or a "hogback." Such a back is strong, but it causes the saddle to slide forward onto the wither and is often accompanied by a crooked hind leg and a too-sloping croup.

COW-HOCKED: The points of the hocks are turned in toward each other, and the horse is likely to "wing in" behind and inter-fere. The lower part of the hock should have great width and breadth and meet an equally strong hind cannon. If it doesn't, the horse is said to be "tied-in below the hocks."

CURBY HOCKS: Very common in jumping horses, and usually results from a horse's being sickle-hocked. A long-cannoned horse is likely to have tendon trouble, and a sickle-hocked horse is likely to develop curby hocks. A horse sometimes has "rough hocks," and this is a forerunner of curby hocks. But, as I say, many fine jumping horses have this defect, and it is not serious in that it does not affect the safety or comfort of the rider, although it is a mark against the horse if he is showing.

SLAB-SIDED: Lacking curvature of the back ribs. A slab-sided horse lacks in stamina.

LONG-COUPLED: A long-backed horse. While a jumping horse that is long-coupled has more extension and is apt to be smoother over jumps, he is also more likely to tire easily on long rides, which makes him somewhat less desirable as a hunter, or weight carrier and easy keeper.

COON-FOOTED: A horse is said to be "coon-footed" when he has unusually long, sloping pasterns. A "coon-footed" horse is generally a pleasant ride, with good, springy gaits, but he tends to break down more easily, since too much strain is placed on the tendons. At the other extreme, the horse with a short, stumpy pastern usually has, also, a short, stiff, stilted gait. This increases the possibility of joint injury because of the increased concussion absorbed in the bony column. The normal slope of the fore pastern to the horizontal is about fifty to fifty-five degrees.

FOOT: The size of the horse's foot should be in proportion to the size of the horse. The heel should always be broad and of moderate height. Low, weak heels are always a source of trouble. The hoof should never be narrow and elongated like the foot of a mule. The sole should have a moderate degree of concavity and the frog should be prominent and elastic. When the foot is too small, the horn of the hoof is often brittle, the base of support is insufficient, and the size is inadequate to absorb the concussion properly. But a too-large foot means an awkward gait. The horse inclines to be clumsy; stumbling and interfering are likely to occur.

SPLAY-FOOTED: A horse that toes out is "splay-footed." Like the horse that toes in, the splay-footed horse, in addition to interfering, is slightly more subject to splints, sidebones, and ringbones than is the horse with a straight foot. Whether the horse toes in or toes out, he is receiving an abnormal amount of concussion in the bony column, due to the uneven distribution of his weight when he lands after a jump. Special shoeing sometimes helps or relieves the condition temporarily.

THE EYES: Should be large, soft, and placed well apart. A horse with a small, deeply set eye is said to be "pig-eyed" and this conformation fault is often associated with a mean disposition. While I have rarely found this to be true, it *is* true that a horse with unusually prominent eyes often has a strongly convexed eye, which tends to be a near-sighted eye and results in shying.

TO SUMMARIZE CONFORMATION: The things for the average rider to know about his horse are those things which may result in an uncomfortable ride or an unsound horse. The beginner should always be on a quiet horse and, if possible, one so constructed that his gaits are smooth and easy to sit to, avoiding the horse with a high, rough trot or one who gives the rider too great a thrust going over a jump. Later on, when the jumps get higher, a straight-shouldered horse is the one to avoid when possible. A straight-shouldered horse is one that will not, as a rule, jump in stride. Because he cannot extend his forelegs enough, the straight-shouldered horse will jump, then hesitate for the merest fraction of a minute on the other side of the fence before galloping on. Unless he's ridden strongly, he also tends to get in underneath his fences and climb, which makes him a harder horse on which to get, and keep, a good jumping position.

Remember, too, that any one, or any several of these faults does not condemn a horse. Avoid them when and if you can, but a horse may have any number of these faults and still be a very good horse for you to own or ride, if he has enough good points to overcome the bad points.

THE HORSE AND HIS UNSOUNDNESSES

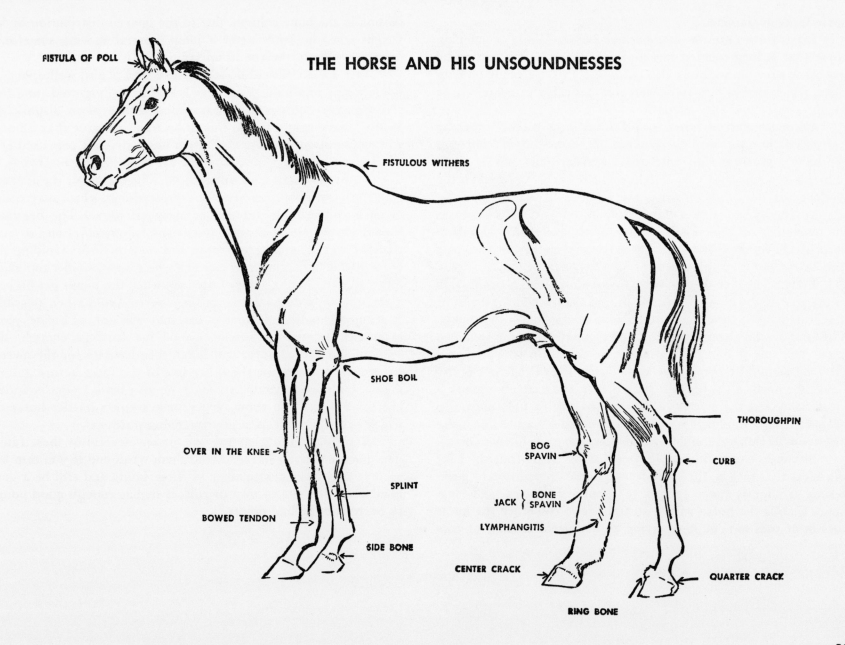

FISTULA OF POLL

FISTULOUS WITHERS

SHOE BOIL

THOROUGHPIN

OVER IN THE KNEE

BOG SPAVIN

CURB

SPLINT

JACK } BONE SPAVIN

BOWED TENDON

LYMPHANGITIS

SIDE BONE

CENTER CRACK

QUARTER CRACK

RING BONE

19

Chapter II

THE HORSE AND HIS UNSOUNDNESSES

When your horse has gone unsound, or when he appears to be ill, the thing to do is to call in a veterinary, and promptly. The illustration and explanation of the unsoundnesses of the horse which I am giving you here, is simply to guide the average horse owner, and make him more alert to the kinds of unsoundnesses which may attack his horse.

A sick horse should not be worked. Horses don't "work out of" unsoundnesses, though older horses do work out of rheumatic stiffnesses and appear to be sounder as they are exercised. Sometimes, an unsoundness becomes "set" as in the case of a bowed tendon. The horse may then go on and work, but his serviceability has definitely been impaired; he has lost some of the elasticity which he needs for jumping; and his showing days are about over.

Whether the sick horse should return to work, when he should return to work, and what kind of work he may safely be expected to do, are all questions which only a qualified veterinarian should even attempt to answer.

Few animals are free from unsoundness, but a horse is serviceably-sound when the unsoundness is not of a type, or a degree, to impair the horse's ability to perform. Small splints, wind puffs, or a small white spot on the cornea, are all unsoundnesses that do not impair the horse's serviceability.

Following is a list of the more common unsoundnesses, their definition, and their description. By comparing this list with the accompanying chart, you will quickly see the part of the body which is attacked and the physical appearance of the individual unsoundnesses:

PERIODIC OPHTHALMIA: Commonly known as "Moon blindness." Can be either acute or chronic, attacks the whole eye, recurring at more or less frequent intervals and usually resulting in total blindness after several attacks. During the attack, the eye is swollen, the cornea is white or cloudy, tears flow freely, and the eyelids are closed to keep out light. The cause is unknown, but it is wise to consider this disease contagious.

FEATHER: Is a white scar on the transparent cornea, and is not serious unless the scar is such as to interfere with the horse's vision.

FISTULA OF THE POLL: Or "Poll evil." A swelling in the region of the poll, which eventually abscesses and often discharges pus through one or more openings. Caused by an injury.

WIND-BROKEN: Or "Windy." A condition more frequently found in big horses, but may attack any horse. It becomes noticeable when the animal is galloped for any length of time, and is characterized by the slightly roaring sound of wind being drawn *into* the lungs. It may result from sudden and excessive overwork, diseases such as pneumonia and influenza. Operations are sometimes successful, but a horse is generally rendered unfit for any work that calls for long gallops, such as hunting, hunter trials, and Olympic riding.

FISTULA OF THE WITHERS: A swelling in the region of the withers, followed by an abscess which may discharge pus through one or more openings. A difficult condition to treat, and even when the active infection has been healed, the scar tissue which results from this type of infection often leaves the animal stiff in the shoulders.

SWEENY: A paralysis of one or more of the muscles covering the shoulder blade. Since it is usually caused by an injury to the large nerve of these muscles, it is a condition found more often in draft horses than in riding horses.

SHOE BOIL: Otherwise known as a "capped elbow." A serious enlargement on the point of the elbow, caused by bruising with a long-heeled shoe while lying down, or by being allowed to lie down in a stall with insufficient bedding.

KNEE SPRUNG: Or "over in the knee." Sometimes a congenital unsoundness, sometimes caused by a tendon injury or an inflammation of the knee joint. Young horses are frequently knee sprung, but will usually straighten up with proper care. In older horses this condition is often a result of a horse tied-in below the knee, which predisposes him to inflammation and a shortening of the flexor tendon.

BOWED TENDONS: An unsoundness frequently found in race horses and resulting from the terrific strain placed on the tendons as the horse leaves his position at a dead gallop. Also caused by a horse jumping out of thick mud or other heavy going. It is characterized by a chronic thickening of the flexor tendons or the suspensory ligament in the cannon region, and is considered a serious defect.

SPLINT: A localized bony growth along the inside of the cannon bone. They often cause lameness while they are forming, but once the splint has set, the lameness disappears. Splints seldom develop on animals over ten years old and usually appear before the horse is seven years old.

BUCKED SHIN: A bony enlargement on the front surface of the cannon bone. Another condition often found among young race horses, and the result of unusual concussion in the bony column. After the acute inflammation has subsided, the bony enlargement which is left seldom causes lameness.

RINGBONE: A bony enlargement in the region of the pastern. It may appear on the long pastern bone, the short pastern bone, or both. In the more severe cases, the enlargement may completely ring the bone. Small and weak pasterns, particularly those that are short, upright and stumpy, are especially prone to ringbone, which is caused by sprains, blows, wounds, or concussion. Not all ringbones cause permanent lameness but in most cases the lameness is both severe and permanent, resisting all forms of treatment.

SIDEBONE: A bulging of both the coronary band and the hoof wall over the affected cartilage. A condition which affects the forefeet almost exclusively, causing lameness while the condition is coming on but permitting the horse to go back to work again as soon as the sidebone is set.

ENLARGED SESAMOIDS: A bony enlargement on the back surface of the fetlock joint. The enlargement is caused by a chronic inflammation of the cartilage that surrounds the sesamoid bones, causing the cartilage to ossify and resulting in a roughening of the smooth articular surface and the groove for the flexor tendons. This is a serious unsoundness, and one that usually causes an incurable lameness in the horse.

QUARTER CRACK: A fracture of the wall at the quarter. The pinching of the sensitive laminae in the crevice, and the resulting inflammation, cause a painful lameness. Contracted heels, dry feet, concussion, and fast work on hard roads may cause this condition.

TOE CRACK: A fracture of the wall at the toe, resulting from improper nailing and a dry, brittle condition of the horn.

NAVICULAR: An inflammation of the navicular bone. Concussion from high action, straight shoulders and pasterns, and much work on hard ground are the principal contributing causes. The symptoms are lameness, stumbling, and stilted gaits, finally reaching a stage where the horse refuses to move forward at all. One of the most difficult of the unsoundnesses to diagnose, and usually only discovered through a process of elimination.

DROPPED SOLE: A flattening of the sole which produces chronic lameness. The wall of such a foot is generally wavy and often concave at the toe when viewed from the side, since it is a foot which has been subjected to chronic attacks of laminitis.

CORNS: Usually the result of bad shoeing, and often producing severe, although very temporary, lameness.

THRUSH: A disease which attacks the frog of the foot and may even destroy it altogether if not detected and treated in time. It is one of the easiest diseases to detect, and one of the most unnecessary, since it is generally the result of carelessness and neglect.

KNOCKED-DOWN HIP: A fracture of the external angle of the hip bone, the affected hip being lower than the normal one. The condition is most easily detected when standing directly in back of the animal.

STRINGHALT: An unsoundness whose cause no one has been able to prove or to define. It occurs more frequently in old animals, does not render the horse unserviceable, and is manifested by a spasmodic flexion of the hock which is most noticeable when the horse is first taken from the stable or asked to back.

CAPPED HOCK: A fibrous enlargement on the point of the hock, often caused by bruises resulting from stable kicking and seldom causing lameness.

BONE SPAVIN: Or "Jack." A bony enlargement on the inside and lower portions of the hock joint. May be caused by faulty conformation, or sprain, or concussion. The resultant lameness is caused by a roughening of the articular surfaces of the lower hock bones. Many horses have spavins and suffer no lameness from them, but the defect constitutes a potential source of lameness.

BOG SPAVIN: A distension of the joint capsule of the hock joint, seen at the inner and upper portions of the front of the hock. Seen most frequently in horses with rather straight hocks, it does not cause lameness except occasionally, in the acute stages.

THOROUGHPIN: A distension of the synovial sheath of the deep flexor tendon which causes a fluctuating swelling on both sides just in front of the point of the hock and beneath the tendon of Achilles. Small thoroughpins show a bulging on the outside only and are commonly found in coarse or common bred horses that have worked hard. The condition is not apt to cause lameness unless some unusual strain brings on an extension of the sheath.

CURB: A chronic thickening of the flexor tendon sheath and plantar ligament on the back border of the hock. When viewed from the side, the back line of a curby hock appears rounded instead of straight. It seldom causes lameness.

SUMMARY: Lameness is a symptom, not a cause. Lameness in a horse is something that should be investigated promptly. A horse's lameness is the outer manifestation of some functional or structural disorder. Any of these unsoundnesses which I have listed here may be the cause of your horse's lameness, and knowing what to look for, and where to look for it, may help you discover the cause of his unsoundness. But treating that unsoundness should always be left to the veterinarian, not to the grooms or to well-meaning friends.

Chapter III

THE MORE COMMON DISEASES WHICH
AFFLICT THE HORSE

To have a bright, glossy coat, to look well and to perform well, a horse must be kept in good physical condition. Some of the more frequent and debilitating diseases to be on guard against:

COUGHS AND COLDS: Always contagious, coughs and colds can spread rapidly through a stable. The horse with a cold should be put in isolation immediately, and the veterinary called at once. The cold itself may not seem important, but such serious illnesses and unsoundnesses as windiness, distemper, and strangles may all result from the untended cold.

MANGE AND RINGWORM are also highly infectious, and grooming equipment used on infected horses must not be used on healthy horses. The veterinary will supply a salve for these diseases, and while they are unsightly and should be treated, they are not serious.

AZOTURIA is a disease which attacks horses that have not been given normal and regular exercise, and are suddenly exposed to vigorous or strenuous work. It is most likely to occur during cool or cold weather. Increased excitability, profuse sweating, and rapid breathing are the first symptoms. Soon, the horse begins to stiffen in his hindquarters, drag the hind legs, and knuckle over in the hind fetlocks. Keep the horse standing, if possible, blanket, give a laxative, and keep the horse on bran mashes, grass, and hay for a few days.

COLIC can be detected by the horse's lying down, rolling, and nosing his belly. The danger here, of course, is to help keep the animal from getting cast in his stall. It is often caused by overeating, eating while fatigued, working too soon after eating, or watering while exhausted. Wind-sucking is another frequent cause of colic. It is well to say here, I think, that all riders should remember that the horse has a small stomach. He should not be fed too much at one time, or fed when he comes in exhausted from a long ride. When horses come in from a hunt, they should be fed a hot bran mash.

These simple precautions will prevent a good many cases of colic, but if your horse does develop colic, blanket him, keep him warm, and send for the veterinarian immediately. After an attack of colic withhold all feed for at least twelve hours.

These are the every-day, common diseases that afflict most horses at one time or another. They need not be serious if the veterinarian is sent for and simple remedies, such as those suggested here, applied to keep the animal reasonably comfortable, until he gets there.

STABLE VICES

The most common stable vices are:

WIND SUCKING: A wind sucker is hard to keep in condition, since he sucks wind into his stomach and can get colic easily as a result. This habit can be helped by the use of a cribbing strap.

CRIBBING: The edge of the manger or any other projection is grasped between the teeth and gradually bitten away. The habit is, unfortunately, not confined to the stable but may be practiced whenever the opportunity offers. A smooth finished stall in which there is nothing to offer a tooth-hold, or the use of a cribbing strap, which compresses the larynx when the head is flexed but causes the horse no discomfort when he is not indulging in this vice, are the two ways to stop cribbing.

WEAVING: A rhythmical shifting of the weight from one front foot to the other. As a rule, lack of regular work and exercise is the cause; and a straight stall plus regular exercise will correct this habit.

KICKING: A great many horses which never show any inclination to kick anywhere else, somehow acquire the habit of kicking in their stalls. Padding the stall with salvaged mattresses will keep the horse from injuring himself, and hobbling one hind leg for a short period of time will sometimes effect a cure.

Chapter IV

THE HORSE'S COLORS AND MARKINGS

Whether you are entering your horse in a show, filling out his thoroughbred papers or just describing him to a friend, you will want to be sure to use the proper terms in describing his individual coloring and marking. Here is a list of markings, colorings and characteristics by which a horse may be identified:

BLACK: A coat of uniform black hairs, a black muzzle.

BROWN: Almost rusty black and distinguished from the black horse by the reddish or mouse-colored muzzle.

CHESTNUT: A medium golden or copper color.

LIVER CHESTNUT: A cinnamon shade, bordering on brown.

BAY: A reddish color of medium shade.

GRAY: A coat of mixed white and dark-colored hairs, about equal in number.

LIGHT GRAY: A shade of gray in which white hairs predominate.

DARK GRAY: A shade of gray in which dark hairs predominate.

IRON GRAY: A bluish gray.

FLEA-BITTEN GRAY: A dark gray coat intermingled with small patches of whitish hairs.

ROAN: A coat of red, white, and black hairs, usually red and white on the body with black mane and tail.

BUCKSKIN: A coat of uniform, yellowish-colored hairs.

PIEBALD: A coat divided into patches of white and black.

PIED BLACK, PIED BAY, AND PIED ROAN, means patched coats of white and black, white and bay, or white and roan.

DAPPLE: Prefixed to any color when spots the size of a silver dollar, and either lighter or darker, overlay the basic color.

THE MOST COMMONLY SEEN MARKINGS ON A HORSE ARE:

STAR: A clearly defined area of white hairs on the forehead.

RACE: A narrow white stripe down the face.

SNIP: A white mark between the nostrils.

BLAZE: A broad splash of white down the face.

WHITE FACE: The horse's face is white from forehead to muzzle.

WHITE CORONET: Or white pastern.

QUARTERSTOCKING: White extending upwards from the coronet to and including the fetlock.

HALFSTOCKING: The white is midway between fetlock and knee, or hock.

THREE-QUARTER-STOCKING: The white is well up the cannon region.

FULLSTOCKING: The white has reached or included the knee, or hock.

Black Points: Black mane, tail, and extremities.

Ray: The line found along the back of some horses.

Zebra Marks: The dark, horizontal stripes seen on the forearm, knee, and back of the cannon region.

HOW TO MEASURE YOUR HORSE

The height of a horse is measured in hands, and a hand is four inches. The measuring stick is placed against the highest point of the withers, with the crossbar resting firmly on the withers and the upright perpendicular.

A good height for a hunter is sixteen hands.

A horse's *bone* measurement is the circumference of the middle of the fore cannon region. A horse's bone is measured in inches. Seven inches is a small bone measurement in any horse over 14/2, and nine inches is an exceptional measurement even in a seventeen hand horse. The bone measurement for the average sixteen hand hunter should be about 8½ inches.

Bone measurement is important. A horse with good bone has a better than average chance of standing up under the shock and concussion to which the hunter and jumper are exposed.

AGE DETERMINATION

Determining a horse's age is something else that is better left to the veterinarian. If you have a thoroughbred horse, with papers, you won't have to worry about his age. If you are buying a half or three-quarter bred horse, the vet who passes him for soundnesses will verify his age.

Other than that, a quick rule-of-thumb method for determining the age of a horse is as follows:

At Five: The horse has a full mouth, with all his cups.

At Six: He loses the cups in the centrals.

At Seven: The cups in the laterals are shallow or have disappeared. The seven-year notch appears on the upper corner incisor.

At Eight: The corner cups begin to disappear although they may remain as a shallow cup until about eleven years of age. The dental star usually appears in front of the enamel ring as a rather long, faint yellow transverse line.

At Ten: Galvayne's groove is distinct and the teeth are becoming more triangular.

At Fifteen: Galvayne's groove is halfway through the corner teeth, and the angle of incidence starts.

At Twenty-Two: Galvayne's groove is extending the length of the tooth, the dental star is large and distinct, and the angle of incidence is pronounced.

But the art of estimating a horse's age accurately cannot be learned from a book, and, as I said before, it is something better left to the experts.

Chapter V

GROOMING THE HORSE

Anyone who owns, or ever hopes to own a horse, may be called upon at some time or another to groom him, and it is well to know the safe, proper way to do it. Also, just as a good cook is able to give constructive criticism to anyone who cooks for her, just so the rider who really knows how his horse should be turned out can ask—or even demand—that the groom in charge of his horse clean him properly.

If you happen to be in charge of your own horse, the first thing to know about him is how to lead him out of his stall. So many beginners, especially, are apprehensive about leading a horse. The safe and proper way to lead a horse is simply to walk forward and the horse will follow. The more you try to stay out of the way of his feet, or look back at him, the more chance there is that you will get stepped on.

If the horse is reluctant to move, gently push him off balance to the right hand then immediately move out. If you are leading out with a halter-shank, grasp the shank about six to eight inches from the snap-hook with the right hand and take the bight of the shank in the left. Never wrap the bight, or loop of the halter-shank around the hand or wrist, as the horse may become excited and rear or try to run away, causing serious personal injury.

TO PICK UP A FRONT FOOT

1. Stand with the back to the horse's head and place the inside hand on the horse's shoulder.

2. Bending over, run the outside hand gently but firmly down the back of the leg until the hand is just above the fetlock. Press against the horse's shoulder with the inside hand, thus forcing his weight onto the opposite foreleg.

3. Grasp the tendons just above the fetlock with the fingers and the horse will usually raise his foot. If he does not raise the foot, it can be easily lifted, since all his weight is now carried on the opposite foreleg.

TO PICK UP A HIND FOOT

1. Stand well forward of the horse's haunches, facing to the rear. Gently stroke his back as far as the point of the hip against which the inside hand is placed for support.

2. With the outside foot well advanced, stroke the leg down as far as the middle of the cannon with the outside hand. While the inside hand presses the horse's weight over to the opposite hind leg, thus lightening the foot desired to be picked up, grasp the

cannon with the outside hand just above the fetlock joint, lift the foot directly toward yourself, so that the leg is bent at the hock.

3. Then move to the rear, keeping the hind leg next to your thigh until his inside foot comes opposite his outside foot. The most common fault is holding the foot out to one side of the horse causing him to resist, due to the discomfort of his position.

TO CLEAN OUT THE FEET

Few things about the care and grooming of a horse are as important as seeing that his feet are properly cleaned. Every rider should know enough about his horse to be able to pick up his horse's feet, before setting out on a ride, and be sure that they are properly cleaned out. Much unsoundness and lameness could be prevented by making use of this simple precaution.

To clean out the feet, always work in order: near fore, near hind, off fore, off hind. Grasp the hoof pick in the hand opposite the side on which you are working (i.e., if you are on the near side, hold the hoof pick in the right hand, if on the off side, hold it in the left hand). With the hoof pick supported by the heel of the hand, clean out the foot from heel to toe. It is very important that the commissures and the cleft be thoroughly cleaned out, as these places are the seat of thrush. Care should be exercised in cleaning the cleft that it is not deepened by cutting the horn of the frog. Inspect the feet for thrush, torn frog, loose shoes, etc., while cleaning.

SAFETY PRECAUTIONS AROUND HORSES

The horse is a timid animal and reacts violently when frightened. However, there is no need to be afraid of horses if certain common-sense precautions are used. The reverse of this is true also, that is, if a rider is over-confident or careless in his actions about horses, sooner or later he will be injured.

Safety Precaution Rules:

Always give warning to a horse when you walk up behind it. The horse is always on the defensive. If it suddenly becomes aware of something in rear of it, its immediate instinct, prompted by fear, is either to kick or run. If tied, or confined in a stall, the animal cannot run, so it usually kicks. When a rider is kicked it is usually through his own carelessness in not observing this rule. If it is necessary to approach a horse from the rear, speak to it to warn of your presence. As soon as the animal is aware of you, stroke it gently on the croup, then move calmly to the head, keeping always close into the horse's body.

In any work about a horse, work from a position as near the shoulder as possible. In this way, you cannot be touched by either front or hind feet of the horse.

Always work close to a horse. If this rule is followed, you cannot be struck by the feet, nor will you receive the full force of a kick. This is particularly true when passing around the horse's rear, or in working about the haunches.

Always let the horse know what you intend to do. For instance, when picking up the feet, do not reach for and seize the foot hurriedly, as this will startle the horse and is liable to cause the animal to kick.

Attendants should not be loud or rowdy when about horses. This tends to make a horse jumpy and nervous both on the ground and under saddle. Eventually, some horses will react to this type of conduct by kicking. A sharp tone of voice may be used for checking an animal, but its loudness should never be any more than is required to meet the situation.

USE OF GROOMING EQUIPMENT

The Currycomb: The currycomb is used with a light, circular motion, and its primary purpose is to break up caked mud, dried sweat and matted hair. It is *never* used below the knees on the forelegs, or on or below the hocks on the hind legs, as the horse is very sensitive in these portions due to the bone lying directly under the hide. The above rule will be applied wherever the bone is close to the horse's outer surface, such as the point of the hip, the shoulder, etc. The currycomb should be very carefully used when working about the belly as the skin there is very thin and sensitive. The currycomb is also used to clean the brush as described below. The currycomb will be frequently cleaned by rapping the *side* of it smartly against the heel several times.

The Brush: The brush is the principal tool used in grooming. It should always be held in the hand nearest the horse's head, except when working in difficult spots, such as the inside of the hind legs, down low on the legs, or under the neck. In using the brush, you should stand well away from the animal, keep the arm stiff, and throw the weight of his body against the brush which is applied in straight strokes. In this manner, the bristles of the brush will loosen and remove dirt and scurf from the hide and coat, and stimulate circulation. This is the basic function of grooming and is essential to good health and appearance of the horse.

The brush is cleaned with the currycomb every two or three strokes, the brush being held *over* the currycomb so that the dirt, when loosened, will fall out of the brush. In brushing the belly, apply the brush the way of the hair.

The Grooming Cloth: The grooming cloth is used to wipe the eyes, ears, nostrils, and dock, and to polish off the horse's coat. In working about the head the action must be gentle so as not to excite or irritate the horse, particularly if the animal is head-shy. Care must be used in wiping out the eyes and nostrils in order that these organs will not be injured. In wiping out the dock the tail should be held about 9 or 10 inches from its root and well elevated with the left hand, using the grooming cloth with the right. Always stand close to and directly in rear of the horse when doing this, so that in case the animal kicks, you cannot receive the full force of the blow. However, if the tail is held high and the grooming cloth used gently the horse will not usually object to this operation. When polishing off the coat apply briskly in the direction in which the hair lies.

TO PICK UP A FRONT FOOT

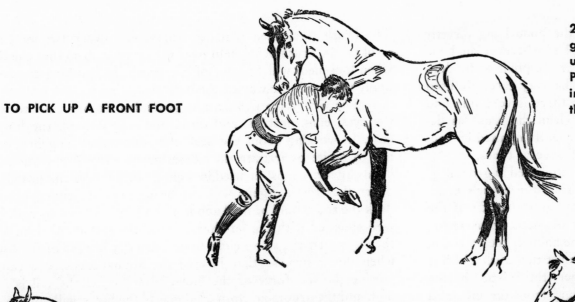

2. Bending over, run the outside hand gently but firmly down the back of the leg until the hand is just above the fetlock. Press against the horse's shoulder with the inside hand, thus forcing his weight onto the opposite foreleg.

1. Stand with the back to the horse's head and place the inside hand on the horse's shoulder.

3. Grasp the tendons just above the fetlock with the fingers and the horse will usually raise his foot. If he does not raise the foot, it can be easily lifted, since all his weight is now carried on the opposite foreleg.

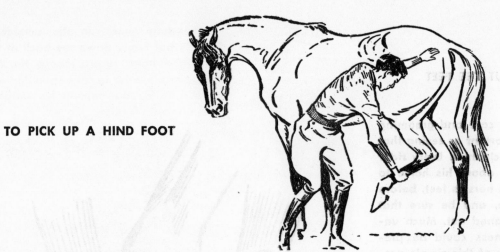

2. With the outside foot well advanced, stroke the leg down as far as the middle of the cannon with the outside hand. While the inside hand presses the horse's weight over to the opposite hind leg, thus lightening the foot desired to be picked up, grasp the cannon with the outside hand just above the fetlock joint, lift the foot directly toward yourself, so that the leg is bent at the hock.

TO PICK UP A HIND FOOT

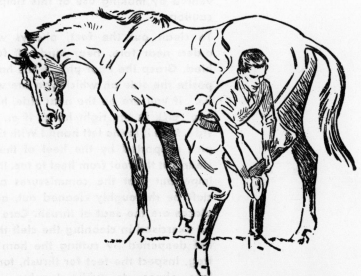

1. Stand well forward of the horse's haunches, facing to the rear. Gently stroke the back as far as the point of the hip against which the inside hand is placed for support.

3. Then move to the rear, keeping the hind leg next to your thigh until his inside foot comes opposite his outside foot. The most common fault is holding the foot out to one side of the horse causing him to resist, due to the discomfort of his position.

33

TO CLEAN OUT THE FEET

Few things about the care and grooming of a horse are as important as seeing that his feet are properly cleaned. Every rider should know enough about his horse to be able to pick up his horse's feet, before setting out on a ride, and be sure that they are properly cleaned out. Much unsoundness and lameness could be prevented by making use of this simple precaution.

To clean out the feet, always work in order: near fore, near hind, off fore, off hind. Grasp the hoof pick in the hand opposite the side on which you are working (i.e., if you are on the near side, hold the hoof pick in the right hand, if on the off side, hold it in the left hand.) With the hoof pick supported by the heel of the hand, clean out the foot from heel to toe. It is very important that the commissures and the cleft be thoroughly cleaned out, as these places are the seat of thrush. Care should be exercised in cleaning the cleft that it is not deepened by cutting the horn of the frog. Inspect the feet for thrush, torn frog, loose shoes, etc., while cleaning.

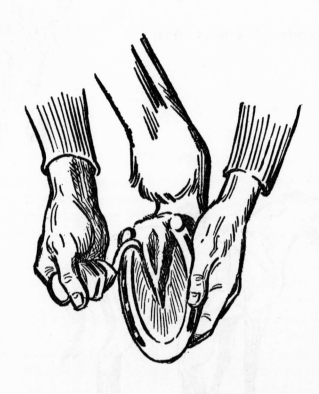

Chapter VI

ARTICLES OF EQUIPMENT AND
THEIR ADJUSTMENT

The rider's comfort and safety will be greatly enhanced by the careful selection of the proper equipment. There are many different types of saddles, of course, and some riders—particularly hunting people—scorn the forward seat, or jumping saddle, while others feel that there's no saddle on earth to be compared with a good, deep, well broken-in Pariani. I must confess that a Pariani is my own choice for a jumping saddle. But the important thing is to choose a saddle in which the rider sits comfortably, and one that's well treed and padded so that there is no friction against the horse's back. As a rule, economy in the purchase of equipment is an extravagance in the long run. The vet's bills for a horse with a sore back will come to a great deal more than the price of a good saddle!

As for bits and martingales, the controversies among grooms, riders and professional horsemen regarding the relative merits of the different types of bits and martingales are endless and never-ending. Let me just say that the bit should fit the horse—both physically and temperamentally. The proper bit for your horse is the bit which he accepts willingly, goes in quietly, and one to which he responds readily.

If you have a horse with a difficult, a bad, or a dead mouth, a good idea is to change the type of bitting fairly frequently. A Pelham and Curb chain act on the bars of the horse's mouth, a snaffle bit works on the cheeks. Therefore, if you switch back and forth, continuing to use a bit of equal severity but one that reacts on a different part of your horse's mouth, you will generally find the horse responding more easily. I prefer this method of handling a difficult mouth to the use of anything as severe as a gag bit or hackamore, both of which can get an inexperienced rider into trouble, and bring on greater difficulties than the rider has sought to overcome.

A few general suggestions about equipment: When showing a hunter in a hack class, *always* use a double bridle or a Pelham. A great many hunter judges will simply refuse to pin a hunter that is shown in a snaffle or single rein bridle in a hack class.

All leather should be kept soft and pliable, both for the sake of the leather itself and the help which this is toward the development of good hands on a horse. It's difficult, to say the least, for a rider to close his hands on the reins, as he should do in controlling his horse, if the reins are stiffened and thickened with dirt.

Bits and stirrup irons should be polished regularly and faithfully. The young horsemanship rider, certainly, should exercise extreme care to see that this is so, as a horsemanship judge will sometimes fault a young rider who appears in the ring on a horse with a rusty bit in his mouth!

Some bits are more severe than others, it is true, but all bits become severe in the hands of the rider who is so insecure or so uncertain that he is constantly going to his reins for support and, therefore, constantly abusing his horse's mouth. For this reason, never use more bit than you absolutely need for controlling the horse.

GENERAL NOTES ON THE USE OF THE CURB BIT: The curb bit is effective through *leverage* rather than pressure. The extent of its severity depends upon the length of the shank: the longer the shank, the more severe the bit. As hunters should not be over-flexed, care should be taken to avoid over-bitting that can cause the horse to become over-flexed and fretful.

The curb bit should not be fixed too tightly in the mouth and must be wide enough to avoid pinching the horse's lips. The curb chain should be twisted until flat, then fitted into the groove in the horse's lower lip. It should be loose enough to form an angle of forty-five degrees with the horse's lower jaw when tension is applied to the rein. A leather lip strap keeps the bit and chain in place. The chain should pass below the snaffle.

The effect of the curb bit is to draw the chin in and bring the head down.

THE WIRE SNAFFLE, which is not illustrated here, is made effective by the same principle as the plain snaffle. Pressure is more severe, but its adjustment is the same as the plain snaffle. Its use is advisable in cases where the plain snaffle does not exert enough control. Many people feel that the wire snaffle is an unusually severe bit, but I can only say again that the severity of any bit in a horse's mouth is in direct proportion to the skill and steadiness of a rider's hands.

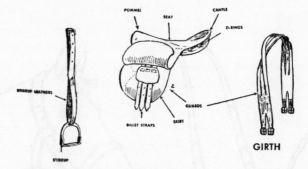

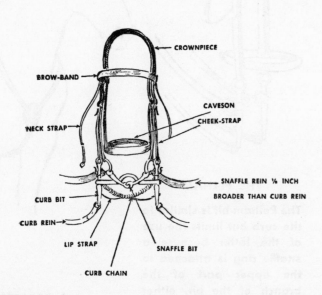

A DOUBLE BRIDLE, or SNAFFLE-AND-CURB, or BIT & BRIDOON

This is a double bridle, also known as a bit-and-bridoon, also known as a snaffle-and-curb. It is used most commonly as a bridle because it has both a snaffle and a curb, so adjusted that they may be used either individually or together, depending upon the effect to be achieved.

ADJUSTMENT OF THE GIRTH

When the girth has been secured, the horse's forelegs should be picked up, first the near and then the off, and gently pulled to the front as far as possible without causing pain or discomfort. This insures a smooth lay of the hair and hide under the girth, and will, to a great extent, prevent, "cinch sores," which are due to the hide being pinched or wrinkled in the strands of the girth, or matted, improperly lying hair. When tightened, the rider should be able to place two fingers between the horse and the girth. This is the correct adjustment.

This is a Hitchcock Girth, good for horses susceptible to girth sores.

ADJUSTMENT OF THE SADDLE

After the saddle has been placed on the horse's back, and prior to letting down the girth, grasp the saddle by the pommel and lightly shake it from left to right three or four times. This will normally settle the saddle in its proper position on the horse and will practically eliminate the possibility of pinched withers due to having the saddle too far to the front.

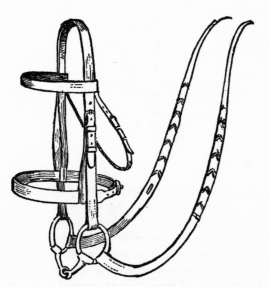

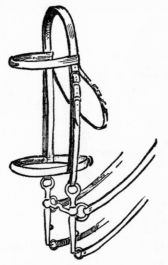

THE PLAIN SNAFFLE

This is the mildest of all bits, acting mainly on the lips. For this reason, it is the least harmful bit, even in the hands of the most inexperienced rider. Its main effect is to raise the horse's head. When adjusting the plain snaffle, fit it snugly into the corners of the horse's mouth, and it is correctly adjusted when a slight pressure on the reins produces a single wrinkle at the corner of the horse's mouth.

HALTER

When a halter is properly adjusted, the crownpiece passes just in the rear of the ears and will remain in that position without slipping. The noseband is in a position on the face two inches below the points of the cheek-bones. The most frequent fault is a position too low. It is important that the loose end of the crownpiece be passed through the buckle and ring as given above, as any loose end of that sort sticking out is liable to be seized by another horse with his teeth, and this is the way many halters are broken!

THE PELHAM

The Pelham bit is similar to the curb but limits the use of the latter because a snaffle ring is attached to the upper part of the branch of the bit, either loosely or as an integral part of the bit. Pelham bits vary in severity according to the length of the shank (which should not exceed six inches for a hunter) and the tension of the curb chain. Obviously, the shorter shank lessens the leverage and force of the curb, therefore the shortest possible shank should be used.

A BREASTPLATE

A breastplate is used mostly on slender horses to prevent the saddle from slipping to the rear. A martingale strap is sometimes attached between the noseband and the ring on the chest. There should be a hand's width between the breastplate and the horse, for proper adjustment.

38

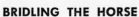

BRIDLING THE HORSE

Take reins in right hand, crownpiece in left hand.

Approach the horse on left side, passing right hand along his neck.

Slip reins over horse's head and let them rest on his neck. Remove halter.

Take crownpiece in right hand and snaffle bit in left hand.

Bring crown piece in front of and slightly below proper position.

Insert thumb into the side of horse's mouth, above tusk, and press upon lower jaw so as to cause him to open his mouth.

Insert bit by raising crownpiece and, with right hand, quietly draw the ears under crownpiece.

Secure throatlatch.

The bridle should be adjusted so that the snaffle bit will touch lightly the upper corners of the lips and so that the throatlatch will admit four fingerbreadths between it and the throat.

A STANDING MARTINGALE

The standing martingale is used primarily to prevent excessively high head carriage which will make the proper effects of the bit impossible. Slow motion films give evidence that the standing martingale does not at any time interfere with the jumping horse if it is not too tight. It may, therefore, be used as often as necessary.

THE RUNNING MARTINGALE

The running martingale is preferred by some because it helps to lower the horse's head through pressure on the bit, viz: The usual effect of a snaffle bit in a horse's mouth is on the cheeks. When a running martingale is used, and adjusted correctly, the pressure of the snaffle is transferred to the *bars*. Any pressure on the bars, brings the horse's chin in, relaxes his jaw, and so tends to lower the head carriage. For this reason, the running martingale can be used with great success by the experienced rider, who knows and understands its function. But the dangers are so obvious, that the running martingale is something which should be avoided completely by the inexperienced rider, or any rider with heavy, or uncertain hands. In the hands of such a rider, the running martingale is applying constant and severe pressure on the bars of the horse's mouth, and may soon be expected to produce a dead-mouthed horse.

PART II

Chapter I

HOW THE HORSE IS TRAINED:
PUNISHMENT AND REWARD

The horse owes most of his aptitude for training to memory. This is something for the rider to bear in mind at all times. Every time the horse is ridden, his "training" begins all over again. While it takes time to un-school a well-schooled horse, every small disobedience on the part of the horse which goes unpunished is helping to un-school, or to sour him.

For instance, the rider begins to "school" his horse for a jump the minute he has settled in the saddle and picked up his reins. From that moment on, the alert or experienced rider is correcting even the slightest resistance on the part of the horse to the demands of the rider.

There is a certain speed at which a horse should walk. Allowing for conformation faults, that speed should be insisted upon. The horse who is allowed to "dog along" at the walk has learned that he can get away with something. His next attempt at disobedience might be trying to break from a trot to a walk, or from a canter to a trot. These things may not seem important at the time, but they build up very quickly to serious disobediences. It is certainly easier, for the beginner, especially, to discipline the horse at the walk or the trot than to wait and have to discipline him at the jump.

Because we do make use of the horse's memory in training

him, the rider *must* be consistent. Decide on what you want from your horse, and insist on getting it. This is one of the many reasons why the rider should take great care not to be over-mounted, since it is almost impossible to punish a horse for a disobedience if you are afraid of him through some form of insecurity. The horse is one of the most eccentric of animals, acquiring either good or bad habits very easily, and seizing swiftly upon any advantage when he sees it.

The rider should take care to differentiate between fear and stubborn resistance on the part of the horse. When the horse is fearful, he should be reassured; when he is offering willful, stubborn disobedience, he should be punished. But one thing for every rider to remember is—*Finish the job*. No matter what it is you start out to do on a horse, from demanding a good, flat-footed walk to negotiating a jump of any size, once you have asked him to do it, don't stop until the horse has yielded to that demand. It is true that this sometimes takes every ounce of courage the rider has at his command; but to give up before the job is finished is to ask for greater trouble later on.

For this reason: Insist on obedience at the slower gaits and stay at the lower jumps until your position in the saddle is secure. Don't allow yourself to be over-mounted!

Don't start something you're not sure you can finish! The resistance built up on the part of the horse is usually out of all proportion to the thing he has been asked to do. If he's allowed to refuse a cross-rail, for instance, without being promptly punished for his disobedience, it won't be long before he is refusing to move forward at all, or exhibiting some other form of resistance.

Many riding and jumping difficulties, and many sour horses, are only the end results of the rider having asked the horse to do something when the rider lacks the knowledge, training, or security to follow through. Ask the horse to do only those things which you know he is capable of doing, and which require no more security in the saddle than you know yourself to have.

REWARD AND PUNISHMENT: The horse is trained through one system which is called the system of reward and punishment.

I don't suppose there is anything in the entire realm of riding which is more misunderstood.

Reward is not confined to feeding your horse the sugar and carrots which he unquestionably enjoys receiving.

Punishment is not necessarily the application of spur or whip to his sides.

Reward is *lack* of punishment.

When the rider's legs close against his horse, asking him to move forward, that is punishment. When the horse obeys that command, the legs relax. That is his reward.

To decrease the gait, the rider's hands close on the reins, adding pressure to a steel bit in the horse's mouth. That is punishment. When he comes down to the gait you want, the feel is instantly relaxed. That is his reward.

When a horse runs out on a fence, the sharp use of the rein with pressure on the bit, turning him in the opposite direction from that in which he attempted his run-out, is punishment. Presented at the fence again, if he takes it, his lack of punishment is his reward.

When the horse refuses a jump, he is punished with legs, spur, or whip, depending upon the temperament and training of the horse. Ridden down to the fence again, if he takes it, the lack of punishment is his reward.

Riders are often seen caressing horses which are completely insubordinate and disobedient. On the other hand, riders who do not realize the amount and degree of punishment inflicted on a horse through bad or jerky hands, through legs that squeeze a horse's sides asking for an increase in the gait while at the same moment the hands exert a stronger and stronger pressure on his mouth asking for a *decrease* in the gait, are guilty of constantly punishing a horse who is doing his best to obey. One extreme is as bad as the other. Both extremes will result in sour, disobedient horses.

A horse's back is an extremely delicate and sensitive part of his anatomy. The rider who comes back on his horse in mid-air over a fence is punishing his horse severely. A horse will fight this particular form of unjust—and unwitting—punishment either by coming down on the jump behind and pulling down a rail, or bringing his head up in the air in an effort to escape and relieve the pressure on his back.

A horse is trained through a system of reward and punishment. So don't reward the horse who has disobeyed, and don't unwittingly punish the horse who is trying to obey!

Never hit a horse on the head! It is a needless form of abuse, and the best it can do is to make a horse head-shy.

When learning to jump, the considerate rider will use either the horse's mane or a neck-strap to avoid banging the horse in the mouth. There is no disgrace in this, and it's an excellent way to train the rider's hands to move forward, while at the same time saving the horse's mouth. A good axiom to remember when learning to jump is, "Better the mane than the mouth."

Punishment should be inflicted *immediately* after a disobedience. The horse is incapable of associating reward and punishment with an act of obedience or disobedience unless such reward or punishment is given immediately. Even a minute late is too late.

Never attempt to punish a horse when you have lost your temper. Such punishment is always bound to be too severe.

Never punish a horse who has disobeyed through ignorance, fear, or faults in his conformation. Be sure the horse knows what you expect of him; be sure his training and conformation are such that he is capable of doing what is asked of him before punishing him.

Don't punish a horse for shying. Take him quietly up to the object from which he is attempting to shy away, show it to him, let him see that he has nothing to fear from it. Punishing will only increase his nervousness and fear.

And last, but certainly not least, let the rider bear in mind that punishments are rarely necessary. Most forms of disobedience on the part of the horse come from the rider's inability to convey his desires to his horse.

All horses like carrots and sugar, but considerate treatment on the part of the rider is something they like—and respond to —even more.

Chapter II

LEARNING HOW TO LEARN

Psychologists and educators tell us that people learn very little, and very slowly, after they have reached the mental age of twelve. But while it is true that children and very young people learn to ride more quickly and more easily than older people, this is usually because children find it easier to concentrate on what they are told. The tired businessman with many worries on his mind, the busy mother, the apprehensive wage-earner who is actually worrying more about falling off than about learning how to ride, must be taught to concentrate. The hardest thing for any riding instructor to do is to get his pupil to take his mind off everything but the immediate objective: When you are learning to keep your heels down, forget about your hands; when you are learning to put your horse into a canter, forget, for the time being, about the correct lead.

And when you are learning—*Don't look!* Keep your eyes up, focused on some point straight ahead of you. To look down throws the entire body out of balance. Form a mental picture of the thing you are to do, and the result you are to achieve, and then, with your eyes up, *feel*.

There is no other way for riding habits to become automatic reactions. When the eyes are up, the mind is functioning and registering reactions. You learn to sense, or feel, when a horse is getting ready to refuse or run out on a jump, to *feel* when he is about to decrease speed and break his stride; and—most important of all for anyone who wants a smooth, safe performance over fences—you learn to *feel* when your horse is about to take off. For as long as the rider has to guess about when his horse is going to take off, he is going to be left back three times out of five.

Learning to feel a horse's responses to your commands at the slow gaits develops that feel which becomes an automatic and valuable reaction later on.

So when you are learning, resist all temptation to look down. Don't look at the jump, don't peer underneath your horse's belly to see which lead he is on. In the learning and beginning stages of riding, when the rider should be mounted on very quiet, safe horses anyway, it is better to make a dozen rounds of the ring on the wrong lead than to look down and see what lead you are on. When you lose a stirrup, don't look for it, *feel* for it. Keep your leg in position and your eyes up, and your foot will find the stirrup more quickly than if you look for it.

DO ONE THING AT A TIME:

Until your reactions on a horse have become instinctive and automatic, don't clutter your mind with half a dozen different things. By concentrating on one thing at a time until it *is* automatic, requiring no further conscious thought, and then going on to master something else, the rider will learn more quickly and be less apprehensive, especially during the early lessons.

Apprehension is based on fear, and fear is based on ignorance. The rider who doesn't know how to stop a horse cannot be expected to show a great deal of courage about getting him started. The rider who doesn't know why his horse refused a jump is naturally apprehensive about riding him down to the same jump again. Since his reluctance is quickly transmitted to the horse, another refusal may safely be expected, and with it, an even more apprehensive, or timid, rider.

That is why the early work, in learning how to ride, must not be hurried either by the over-anxious pupil or the overzealous parent. It is easier to prevent the formation of bad habits, either in a horse or in a rider, than to correct them. The young child, mounting a horse or pony for the first time, shows no fear. It is only bad experiences on a horse that produce fear and timidity, and most of these bad experiences can be avoided.

THE PUPIL SHOULD: Never be apologetic about low fences or quiet horses.

Have confidence in his instructor, or get another in whom he *can* have confidence.

Allow himself to be told what to do, not tell the instructor what he wants to do or *how high he knows he can jump if his instructor will only let him.*

Follow a definite sequence of instruction, lesson-by-lesson and grade-by-grade, such as I have worked out in this book.

Be sure one lesson has been mastered thoroughly before moving on to the next lesson; and be sure the quiet horses have been mastered *thoroughly* before risking confidence and security —to say nothing of riding pleasure and relaxation—by asking for the more difficult horses.

THE INSTRUCTOR SHOULD: Never ridicule a pupil's horse,

riding ability or past experience.

Consider a rider's good and bad conformation points in much the same way as he would consider a horse's conformation: There are some conformation faults which limit a rider's ability just as there are conformation faults that limit a horse's ability.

Realize the importance of temperament. There are temperamental people, just as there are temperamental horses. Even if the pupil has proved that he is physically capable of taking the bigger fences, he should not be urged to do so if he is temperamentally unsuited to the increased nervous tension which naturally accompanies the higher jumps and the more difficult kinds of riding. To ridicule such a pupil, in the mistaken notion that you are appealing to his pride to do what his heart won't do, is as unkind as it is unwise.

Try to avoid having a negative attitude. By this I mean, add to what the pupil already has, instead of trying to start all over again. He *has* a certain horse, he *has* a certain seat, both acquired, as a rule, at considerable expense. It is extremely discouraging to be told he has to get rid of his horse and "forget" everything he has learned. The best and most the pupil can do is improve on everything he has learned, and this the conscientious instructor can and should do for him.

Use a regular sequence of instruction, beginning with the correct use of the aids in stopping, then moving on to the correct use of the aids in moving forward and in turning. There can be no seat on a horse until there is control, and no hands until there is a secure seat.

Insist that the early work go slowly. There is absolutely nothing to be gained and everything to be lost by hurrying the early work, since no real progress can be made with even the most talented pupil until security has been achieved.

Chapter III

MOUNTING

1. The rider stands half facing to the rear, opposite the horse's left shoulder. He takes the reins in his left hand, with the little finger between them, and the bight falling to the off side. Adjust the reins so that they give a gentle, even bearing on the horse's mouth. Now, place the left hand, with the reins, on the horse's crest. The rider then places the left foot in the stirrup, assisted by the right hand if necessary, and brings the left knee against the saddle. Without pause, he places the right hand upon the cantle, and rises by an effort of the right leg, aided by the arms. He keeps the left knee bent, and firmly pressed against the saddle, the toe depressed, and the upper part of the body inclined slightly forward in order to keep the saddle from turning.

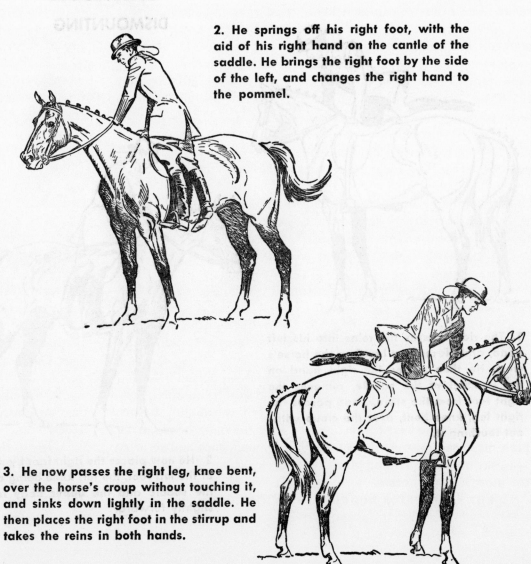

2. He springs off his right foot, with the aid of his right hand on the cantle of the saddle. He brings the right foot by the side of the left, and changes the right hand to the pommel.

3. He now passes the right leg, knee bent, over the horse's croup without touching it, and sinks down lightly in the saddle. He then places the right foot in the stirrup and takes the reins in both hands.

DISMOUNTING

1. The rider passes the reins into his left hand, and places that hand on the horse's crest. He then places the right hand on the pommel of the saddle, removes the right foot from the stirrup, and passes the right leg, knee bent, over the croup without touching it.

2. He now places the right foot by the side of the left foot, the left knee being against the saddle and the upper body inclined slightly forward.

3. He puts the weight of his body on his hands, removes the left foot from the stirrup, then descends lightly to the ground.

Chapter IV

POSITION

A good position on a horse is one that can be adjusted to the needs of the rider, and one that fulfills the two primary requisites of a good seat on a horse: A seat that provides a maximum of security for the rider, and a minimum of interference with the horse.

The position which you see illustrated here amply fills those two basic requirements.

Quite obviously, if our sole aim were to provide maximum freedom for the horse, the stirrups could be shortened drastically, taking even more weight off the horse's back and putting the rider more or less in the position of the jockey on a race horse.

If our sole aim were to provide maximum security for the rider, the stirrups could be drastically lengthened, giving the rider more leg on a horse.

Both these modifications of the seat have severe drawbacks: In the first, the rider has no security at all, and rides, like the jockey, entirely on balance. In the second, the horse's movements are so severely interfered with, by the pounding of the rider's weight on his back and against his mouth, that his work is made doubly hard, with resultant loss of efficiency and good performances.

Therefore, the ideal position on a horse is one that allows the rider full use of all his natural aids—such as the calves of the legs, the inside of the thighs to and including the inner bones of the knees, and the hands—by placing them in positions where they serve to increase the rider's security in the saddle while at the same time acting as a means of communication between the horse and rider.

Anyone who has ever been privileged to observe the horse turned loose in pasture, galloping down to a fence, knows that the free horse doesn't fall over his fences, "get in wrong," or commit any of the other blunders which occasionally make jumping a hazard. All such faults and disasters are generally the result of interference on the part of the rider with the horse's movements. There is some interference which cannot be helped, regardless of the rider's skill or his position in the saddle. A horse stumbles, or shies suddenly just before a fence, and the rider is temporarily thrown out of position. But it is safe to say that a majority of the falls and refusals occurring at horse shows, result from severe—and sometimes constant—interference with the horse due to the rider's faulty or unbalanced position in the saddle.

The position which you see illustrated here is the position which I teach and advocate because it avoids extremes, and it has

THIS IS A CORRECT POSITION

The rider's body is distributed as follows:

Part of the Body	Definition	Position
1. Upper Body	All parts of the body from the hips up.	Eyes up, shoulders back; hands over and in front of horse's withers; knuckles thirty degrees inside the vertical; hands, three inches apart and making a straight line from horse's mouth to rider's elbow.
2. Base	All parts of the body in contact with horse or saddle.	In the center of the saddle; inside of thighs to and including inner bones of knees and legs.
3. Leg	All parts of the leg from the knee down.	Toes out, fifteen to forty-five degrees according to rider's conformation; ankles flexed in, heels down, calf of leg in contact with horse and slightly behind girth.
4. Equilibrium	Balance of upper body over the base of support at the different gaits.	At the walk, vertical; slow trot, slightest possible forward inclination of the upper body; posting trot, inclined forward; canter, half way between the posting trot and the walk; galloping and jumping, same inclination as the posting trot.

the added advantage of putting the rider into a correct jumping position long before he has even begun to walk over a rail on the ground.

I don't believe that the average rider has a lifetime to spend learning the fine technicalities of horsemanship. Therefore, in so far as it is commensurate with a rider's safety and a horse's well being, I plan the lessons so that the rider is enjoying the thrills and pleasure of jumping the low fences within a comparatively *very* short time. For the higher fences, the *rider* does exactly the same things which he does on the lower fences. The difference is that he must have a somewhat better horse, and he must have spent enough hours in the saddle to have built up the necessary confidence in his instructor, himself, and his horse, to be ready to tackle the higher fences.

Throughout this book, you will observe that I carefully avoid using the word *"nerve"* in its accepted sense, because, as far as riding is concerned, nerve comes from confidence. When a rider has had enough good experiences on a horse, when he has developed confidence in his instructor, which later can and should be transferred first to the horse and then to the rider himself, *every* rider has nerve. The riders who take chances without understanding the risks involved are more foolhardy than courageous.

For this reason, the pupil who is made to control his natural impatience in the early stages of developing a secure seat on a horse will find himself making incredibly rapid progress later on when this position has become automatic. The reason: higher jumps, faster gaits, require only a very slight change in the forward inclination of the upper body.

You will see, and have seen, a great many fine and outstandingly successful riders in the show ring whose position in the saddle defies everything I have said, or will say to you, regarding position. It is well to bear in mind, however, that there are geniuses in every field, and the field of riding is no exception. Some people have exceptionally well co-ordinated and athletic bodies. They can be any place on a horse, and still manage to be "with" the horse when he takes a jump, by performing truly incredible and amazing gymnastics in the saddle at the last minute.

They do well, and they succeed. Thomas A. Edison also did well, and also succeeded, with almost no formal schooling. The question invariably comes up, though—"How much better might he have done, how much time might he have saved, how many corners might he have cut on his way to the goal he finally reached, if he *had* had the advantage of formal schooling?"

This is equally true of riders—and of horses—who seem to do everything wrong and still succeed, and it is something for every rider to bear in mind when questioning the advisability of learning new, and more modern, riding techniques.

This position utilizes four parts of the rider's body: The Upper Body, which is all parts of the body from the hips up; the Base, which is all parts of the body in contact with horse or saddle; the Leg, which is all parts of the leg from the knee down; and the rider's Balance, or Equilibrium, meaning the balance of the upper body over the base of support.

To take this position in the saddle: The rider should spend the first five minutes of the first fifteen hours of riding adjusting his position in the saddle.

When the different parts of the body have been arranged and distributed as shown and explained in the accompanying illustration and text, let the rider rise in the saddle, placing one hand on the pommel to steady himself. Relax the ankle joints so that the heels, driven by the body's weight, are forced far down, keeping the stirrup straps vertical and the lower legs in place against the horse's sides. The toes turn out naturally, at an angle from fifteen to forty-five degrees, depending upon the conformation of the rider. Then, holding the lower legs in place, *sink* down slowly into the saddle, with the crotch in the middle of the saddle.

Next, try to hold this position at the walk, then the slow, or sitting, trot, and then the posting trot. Just five minutes a day spent taking and holding this position at these three gaits will produce excellent results. At the end of the first fifteen hours of riding which have been preceded by this simple exercise, the rider will find himself assuming this position in the saddle automat-

COMMON DISTORTIONS OF A GOOD POSITION

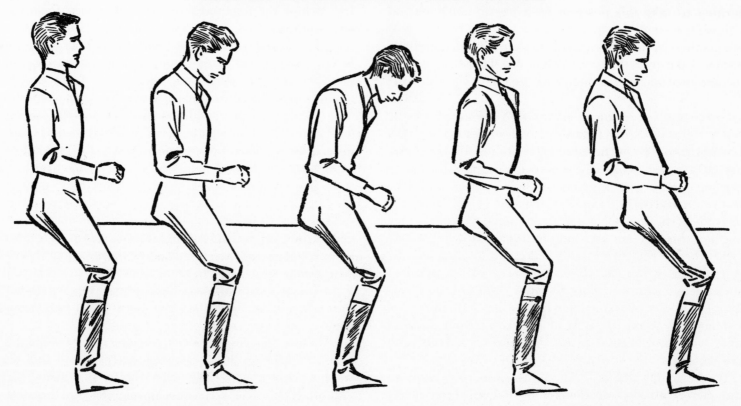

1. Upper body in correct position.

2. What happens to the upper body when the eyes drop.

3. Careless position, a roachback.

4. Too stiff and tense.

5. Buttocks tucked under, knees come up, security is lessened.

ically.

In learning to take this position on a horse, don't look at yourself adjusting your position. Try to do as much of it as possible from a picture which has formed in your mind by studying this illustration. Like everything else connected with this position, learning to take it properly at a standstill prepares the rider for later work.

Adjust your position a step at a time and don't expect to be able to keep it right away. It takes time, but the time actually is shortened by not trying to hurry these early stages, and so avoiding pressure, strain and fatigue.

In learning the correct position of the leg, first study the illustration here; then, with your eyes straight ahead, and at a standstill, say to yourself, "Toes out at an angle of from fifteen to forty-five degrees." Your own leg conformation will pretty much tell you what is the correct and therefore comfortable degree for you. Then, when you think you have it, ask your instructor, or someone who is willing to work with you, to check your position. If you're working alone, a riding hall mirror is almost invaluable. If no mirror is available, adjust your position in accordance with your mental picture of what is correct, and *then* look to compare.

Next, try "ankles flexed in." Again, check in your mind on your mental picture of the ideal ankle flexion as shown here, which calls for the ball of the foot to be in the stirrup—but *resting* there, not pressing—heels down, the calf of your leg slightly behind the girth and in contact with your horse. I have no feeling whatsoever about riding "home" or riding on the ball of the foot; but *when the pupil is learning to keep his heels down, it's easier for him to put weight in the heels if he rides on the ball of the foot.* And *do* remember that pressure and weight is carried in the heel, *not on the stirrup*. Pressing on the stirrup has the effect of drawing the rider's calf away from his horse, thereby depriving him of an important means of communicating with and controlling his horse, and lessening the rider's security in the saddle.

This same procedure, as outlined above, should be followed for each of the four parts of the body which form your position on the horse.

The importance of not looking down as you adjust the different parts of the body cannot be over-stated. Learn from the very beginning to keep your eyes up, to form a mental picture in your mind—whether it is a picture of your position on a horse or a picture of an outside course over which you are to ride. To learn this all-important habit of *looking* and feeling, I recommend that the rider focus his eyes on some point directly ahead of him and on a level with his eyes so that he can catch himself if he glances down. Learning to "ride a line" over a course of very low fences is another excellent exercise for learning to keep the eyes up. It is physically impossible to maintain proper balance in the saddle when the eyes are down. The next time you take a very low fence, try it. First look down at the fence you are taking, and the next time, determine to keep your eyes up. You will be astonished at the difference this makes both in your own position on the horse, *and* the horse's performance over a fence.

When the eyes are down, nothing is functioning. The driver who kept his eyes on the steering wheel would soon find himself and his car in a ditch. The rider who looks down at his horse will soon find his horse refusing and running out, because when the rider's eyes are down, he is *looking* instead of thinking, or feeling. Watching a horse take a fence is a good way *not* to have him take the fence.

To Summarize Position: A good position in the saddle is one that provides security for the rider and freedom of movement for the horse.

The position illustrated here is one that is readily and easily adapted to the requirements of both the hunt field and the show ring. Purely for the comfort of the rider, the stirrups may be dropped when the rider is going out for a long day in the hunt field. But even then, the horse's comfort should be considered to the point of not dropping the stirrups, and thereby shifting the weight backward on the horse's loins and kidneys, any more than is absolutely necessary.

For the higher jumps—by which I mean four feet or more—the stirrups may be shortened, since by this time the rider should have sufficient security in the saddle to be able to sacrifice security to the good performance of his horse over that size fence.

When breaking or schooling very young or green horses, the stirrups may again be dropped, since the rider requires more leg on a horse for schooling green horses.

Remember, when learning this position on a horse, that it is the position which comes nearest to reaching that happy medium of freedom of movement for the horse and security for the rider. There is no such thing as perfection, and everything in life is compromise. We might achieve greater speed or better jumping performance from the horse if we perched up on his withers as the jockey does, and there might be a greater feeling of security if the legs were wrapped around a horse. But to ride well, look well, have a free-moving horse, and still be absolutely secure in the saddle, this position is the best one I know of.

In adjusting the forward inclination of the body for the different gaits and the higher jumps, remember that forward inclination is controlled by the opening and closing of the hip angles, *not* by jackknifing forward, collapsing on the horse's neck, or humping the backbone.

It is the horse's back, loin and hindquarters which furnish the driving power. Another good reason why they should be reasonably unhindered.

The rider should take approximately five minutes of a riding hour to go through a recitation or mental reminder of the four basic parts of this position, then check his position standing still. If the rider will go through this simple exercise for the first five minutes of *every* riding hour, this position will soon become automatic, because it is a simple, and natural, position to assume and one in which the rider will very soon feel comfortable.

Don't try to learn this new position all at once. The temporary loss of security which always accompanies changing old riding habits for new ones, and the slight strain on new muscles being used for the first time, plus any slightest uncertainty on the part of the rider, can all be avoided if the rider will learn this new position by practicing only five minutes a day at a walk, a slow trot, and a posting trot.

Repetition is what actually teaches you—doing the same thing again, and again, and again. And repetition, plus making haste slowly, is what you will find me advocating in this book for everything—from acquiring a good position on a horse to learning how to jump.

Chapter V

THE ELEMENTARY USE OF THE AIDS FOR
THE INCREASE AND DECREASE OF SPEED

Before moving on to the posting trot, or motion of any kind at all, the rider, to be safe and at ease in the saddle, must have at least an elementary knowledge of the aids that are used to increase or decrease a horse's forward motion: what these aids are, and when and how they are applied.

The first aid which the rider is called upon to use the minute he has settled himself in the saddle is the rein aids.

These are your reins, of course, and they are called a *direct rein aid* when the rider has an equal amount of feel, or contact with his horse's mouth, on both reins, as is the case when you are first learning to use your reins to decrease your horse's speed. The "direct rein" is the rein which makes a straight line from the horse's mouth to the rider's elbow.

The inexperienced rider should first learn the use of this rein aid at a walk. The horse is allowed to walk out, while the rider collects the reins sufficiently to have a feel of his horse's mouth. No aid should ever be applied to any horse, under any circumstances, until and unless the rider has a feel of his horse and has his hands in the proper position.

To DECREASE SPEED: Still at the walk, the rider, having established light contact with his horse's mouth, closes his hands on the reins. The little fingers of the rider's hands act strongly, in a squeezing motion, increasing pressure on the reins and, therefore, on the horse's mouth. The horse comes back from the walk to the halt.

To move the horse forward again, or INCREASE SPEED: The rider once again goes through the motions of establishing the contact with his horse's mouth which he has relaxed after the horse has obeyed his command and come down to the halt. With contact once more established, so that the rider will be able to control the amount of forward motion and not get more speed than he desires to get, the legs close in against the horse's sides.

With the well-schooled horse, just closing the legs against his sides is enough to produce forward motion. It is the leg aid which should always be applied first, before stronger methods, or aids, are used. To give a high-strung or nervous horse a boot in the side—as so many, many inexperienced riders are always doing—is to ask for, and usually get, trouble.

If the horse does not move forward in response to the rider's legs closing on him, then the spur, and finally, the whip or riding bat must be resorted to.

The inexperienced rider should *never* be mounted on a horse so sour to the leg that he requires the use of the stronger aids which, if not used judiciously, can cause serious trouble and even injury to the rider. In learning the use of these elementary controls, it is important that they be learned at the very slow gaits, while the rider learns to feel the kinds and degrees of effects which the different aids produce. He should first move only from the halt to the walk and back to the halt again, until the aids needed for this simple motion are functioning smoothly, and until the rider has relaxed as he learns that he can control the speed at which his horse will move out under him.

The rider should *never* kick his horse. It is not only a most unhorsemanlike sight, but it has the effect of kicking the rider out of the saddle, precisely as a lemon seed might be squeezed out by holding the lemon tightly between two fingers and squeezing. Kicking the horse disturbs the rider's balance and equilibrium in the saddle, lessens his safety, and does nothing to teach the horse obedience. When the horse is "sour to the leg," the spur or whip should be used immediately, then the pressure of the legs closing against the horse's sides tried again to see whether, with more severe punishment, he has learned that he must yield to this command.

There are few sights less unhorsemanlike than that of the rider wildly flaying his horse's sides with his legs and heels while the horse, long since immune to such treatment and abuse, stands perfectly still, refusing to move.

USE ALL OF THE AIDS CORRECTLY: When one aid will not produce a desired result, resort to a stronger aid. If the pressure of the legs closing against the horse's sides won't cause him to move forward, the spur or the whip is used. If closing the hands on the reins will not bring a horse down to the desired gait, the rider uses firmer methods, such as the pulley rein, which will be described and explained in a later chapter.

Because these more advanced aids require greater security in the saddle, the rider should not be on a horse that requires their use until his position is *secure*. As I mentioned in an earlier chapter, never ask a horse to do more than you are capable of forcing him to do; and the rider who is just learning to ride, or just learning the correct use and co-ordination of the aids, is certainly not able to insist on obedience from a horse who cannot, or will not, respond to light pressure on the reins or a fairly mild action of the legs. It does not require a good horse to do these things, but it does require a good-dispositioned horse, and that is the kind of horse you should be on at this stage of your riding education.

HANDS

Hands, like reins, are one of the rider's natural aids, and one of the aids he always uses when he is mounted on a horse, whether he is using them voluntarily or involuntarily, skillfully or awkwardly.

Good hands do not always follow a good seat, but good hands are impossible without a good seat. And by a good seat, I mean a seat that is safe enough and secure enough so that the rider never has to go to his reins for support. No horse can be expected to associate the ideas of halting, turning, or decreasing the gait with varying tensions on the reins if tension is applied a hundred times when no such things are meant or wanted.

Horses are born with dispositions that make them either less or more adaptable to training and schooling, it is true, but horses are not born with bad mouths. Bad hands make bad mouths, and bad mouths can, in turn, make heavy if not bad hands in the inexpert rider.

For this reason, until the rider has achieved a fair degree of security in the saddle, he should strive only to have steady hands. These are hands that even the rankest amateur can acquire, and reasonably soon, if he will concentrate not on the far-off goal of educated hands, but on the immediate goal of steady hands.

When the legs have asked for an increase in the gait, the rider should be sure that his hands relax sufficiently to allow the horse's head and neck to move freely to accommodate the increased impulsion. When the hands have closed on the reins, asking for a decrease in the speed, and the horse has obeyed the command, the hands should relax *instantly,* rewarding the horse for his obedience and making him quicker to respond the next time the signal is given.

A rider may have any one of four kinds of hands on a horse: Good hands, by which I mean steady, considerate hands; Bad hands, which are the hands that constantly abuse a horse's mouth by the rider's either intentionally or unintentionally urging forward and reining back at the same time; No hands, referring to those riders who habitually ride with excessivly long reins, maintaining no contact with the horse's mouth at all; and, finally, the goal of every ambitious rider: Educated hands.

It requires almost a lifetime of riding to acquire really educated hands, because by "educated hands" we mean hands which are fixed on the reins with a resistance *exactly* equal to the resistance of the horse's mouth against them, and hands so sensitive that they can yield the very instant the horse yields to their pressure. To continue that severe a pressure in the horse's mouth even an instant longer than is necessary is to continue a punishment *after* the horse has yielded.

Many riders get into the habit of riding with "no hands" through having been cautioned against using too much pressure on a horse's mouth. Too much pressure, produced by the set or heavy hand, is certainly to be avoided, but on the other hand, so is the horse whose mouth "can't be touched." All cars come equipped with brakes, and all horses should, too. There is something wrong with the horse who cannot or will not respond to the proper application of the rein aid, and he's a horse which the young or inexperienced rider, certainly, should not be on.

Until the seat is secure, strive to keep the hands steady, avoid having them bob up and down like a sewing machine while your horse is trotting. Remember that every time your hands bob up and down, you are punishing your horse. The pressure of a steel bit against the horse's mouth is sometimes a necessary punishment, but it is entirely too severe a punishment to be treated lightly or inflicted carelessly.

After security in the saddle has helped the rider to have steady hands, the next step toward the development of good hands is—Passive hands. These are hands that are able to function independently of the body, that can work separately, in sequence, or simultaneously.

Passive and active hands are used simultaneously, for instance, in turning a horse. Turning to the right, the right hand becomes active, the left hand is passive. Many riders *think* their hands are passive when, actually, they are active. It is important to be sure that the passive hand is really passive when the active hand is active. Human beings have nervous breakdowns when they try to go in two directions at once, and yet this physical and mental impossibility is something which the unskilled or thoughtless rider is constantly demanding of his horse whenever he clashes his aids, or controls. The rider is said to be clashing his controls when his hands refuse to yield after the legs have asked for forward motion; or when a passive hand continues to be active, conflicting with the signal of the active hand; or when an unsteady leg against a horse's side continues to ask for forward motion while the hands continue to increase their feel against his mouth, countermanding the unintentional signal of the legs.

The thing to bear in mind in the development of good hands is that they can only follow a secure seat. When learning to ride, forget hands altogether except to take care that the hands are steady enough not to interfere with the horse's mouth and inflict needless pain and punishment. Ride only quiet horses which will respond, either through the medium of a good mouth or a good disposition, to light and proper pressure on the reins which is supplied by *closing* the hands and *not* by pulling on the reins. As the rider's security in the saddle is increased, he should gradually begin to acquire steady hands.

LEGS

Just as there are active and passive hands, so, too, are the legs on a horse either active or passive. Again, care must be exercised to see to it that the passive leg is *really* passive, overseeing the action of the active leg, and becoming active only when the horse decreases the speed at which he is moving.

Some riders have "no legs" on a horse, because their grip is entirely through the knees and the upper thighs. Such a position may be made to be equally secure on a horse through the medium of strength, balance, and general athletic ability, but it is obvious to even the beginner that when the rider does not bring the calves of his legs in against the sides of his horse, he is needlessly sacrificing an important means of control over the horse and part of his security on the horse.

Every rider needs all the security, and all the control over a horse which he can get, so that it seems foolish deliberately and needlessly to sacrifice a part of the seat which provides so much control and which so greatly increases the rider's security.

As with hands, when making a turn, one leg is passive, one leg becomes active. The passive leg must really be passive. While clashing the controls, by allowing the supposedly passive leg to become active, is not too important in the early work, it is forming bad habits for the rider and teaching the horse disobedience, since he cannot possibly respond to two completely opposing and opposed orders at the same time, and usually reacts by responding to neither. These bad habits, so easily acquired in the early stages of riding where they do not show up so glaringly as they do later on, often form the basis for some of the rider's most difficult riding problems.

Horses that have become habitual rearers, horses that lash out with their hind legs, are *very* often only the result of having been ridden by riders who unknowingly clashed their controls. Clashing the controls is a form of injustice to the horse, and the horse will always find some way to fight back.

USE OF THE ELEMENTARY AIDS IN BACKING

A good many horses win hack classes, only to lose them when the judge asks the rider to back his horse. A good many horsemanship riders are 'way up in the ribbons until the judge asks them to back their horses. Then suddenly the rider's hands fly up into the air, up comes the horse's head, and if he backs at all it's in an awkward, jerky way that looks more as though he's stumbling backward than *moving* backward.

The proper way to back a horse, using the elementary aids of direct rein, hands, and legs, is as follows: The rider establishes contact with his horse's mouth by taking a feel on the reins. *Holding* that feel so that the horse cannot move forward, and with the rider's eyes not only up, but focused on some point directly ahead of him, he now closes his legs against his horse's sides.

This method of backing the horse is based on exactly the same, simple theory you use when backing your car. When you shift the car into reverse so that it cannot go forward, and then apply gas, the car moves—backward.

When, by applying pressure against the horse's mouth with the direct rein and *holding that feel,* the rider *then* applies gas, by closing his legs against his horse's sides, which is the signal to move forward, the horse, unable to move forward because of the pressure against his mouth, will start to move back.

The horse, backing, should take regular, even steps; and the rider's legs apply either more or less pressure on one side of the horse or the other as he feels the horse beginning to swing to one side. If the rider is careful to keep his eyes up and focused, as I say, on some definite point ahead of him, he will feel all these movements on the part of the horse as he begins to back, and be able to correct them. To look down at the horse, when attempting to back him, is to have him swing his hindquarters from side to side, because the rider's body is immediately out of balance, and his legs cannot respond to the feel of the horse. In riding, you have *got* to feel. You cannot, and you must not, look. When you look down at your horse all you will see are your own mistakes! To keep from making those mistakes, keep your eyes up and focused on some definite point or some definite object.

I cannot say this often enough. Horses refusing to move forward, fractious horses, horses running out or refusing a fence, horses getting in under their fences, all of these things *can be* and too often are caused by the rider dropping his eyes. The brain cannot function, the body cannot be in balance when the rider's eyes are down!

SPEEDS AT THE DIFFERENT GAITS

Before you take up the posting trot, which is explained in the next chapter, I think you should understand the proper speeds for the walk, the slow or sitting trot, and the posting trot.

At the walk, the horse moves four miles an hour; slow trot, six miles an hour; at the posting trot, eight miles an hour.

The proper speeds at the canter, the gallop, and the different size jumps is something we will take up later. To learn to ride, the rider should have only one thing on his mind at a time. To teach riding, the good instructor will put only one thing on a pupil's mind at one time. For that reason, I am not going to clutter your mind now with speeds at the faster gaits until you are ready for those gaits.

REWARD AND PUNISHMENT

At this stage of your riding knowledge, you can use and should use only the elementary aids which I have described here for rewarding or punishing your horse. When your legs close against his sides asking for an increase of speed, consider this a punishment, even though a necessary one. When he has responded to the pressure by an increase in the gait, immediately relax that pressure. When your hands close on the reins, asking for a decrease, and the horse comes down to the slower gait, be quick to relax the pressure against his mouth.

Simple and even obvious though these things sound, the clashing of these elementary controls produces serious disobediences, souring the horse's sides to the rider's leg and helping to ruin his mouth.

Every time you ride a horse, you are helping either to school or to un-school him. Stay on the horses you can control with ease and security, insist on their obedience to your wishes when you know the horse has understood what it is you are asking of him, and be quick to reward this obedience by relaxing pressure on mouth or sides.

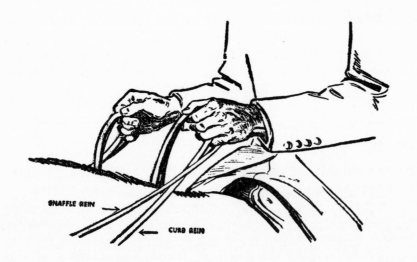

SNAFFLE REIN

CURB REIN

HOLDING DOUBLE REINS CORRECTLY

When the reins are held in both hands, the snaffle rein enters each hand underneath the little finger. The curb enters between the little and ring fingers, both reins run up together, passing through the palms, over the index finger with the thumb on the reins.

HOLDING A SINGLE REIN CORRECTLY

The reins enter the two hands around the little finger, passing up through the palms and over the index fingers. The thumbs are placed on top of the reins, placing them against the middle joint of the index finger, which prevents the reins from slipping. This is also a "direct" rein because it makes a direct line from horse's mouth to rider's elbow.

Chapter VI

THE POSTING TROT

There are three ways of posting to the trot: Ahead of the motion of your horse, with the motion, and behind the motion. There are *two right ways* of posting to the trot: With the motion of your horse, and behind the motion of your horse. But when I say posting behind the *motion,* I do not mean posting behind the *horse.* It is never good horsemanship to post behind the *horse,* nor is it ever correct to post ahead of the *motion* of your horse. Posting ahead of the motion produces an insecure, wholly unbalanced seat on a horse, and unfortunately it is this grotesque, unbalanced position which is constantly being confused with what is meant by posting *with* the motion.

So let us examine the two right ways of posting with the horse and see not only why they are right, but when they are right.

I advocate posting *with* the motion of the horse. So first of all, what do I mean when I say, "With the motion of the horse"? And why do I prefer this method of posting?

When I ask the rider to be with the motion of his horse, I mean that his upper body is to be inclined forward over his base so that he can adjust the forward inclination of his upper body to the horse's trot. Some horses, as we all know, have high or rough trots; some are pony-gaited; some have the smooth, easy gaits. The degree to which the horse thrusts the rider upward and forward is the degree to which the rider's forward inclination of his upper body must be adjusted.

The rider who is in the correct position for posting with the motion, does not have to lean farther forward, producing the absurd exaggerations which are so often mistaken for posting *with* the motion. As the speed, or forward propulsion, of the horse increases, a very *slight* increase in the forward inclination of the rider's body continues him in a secure, easy, correct position.

But one of the most important reasons for teaching this method of posting to the trot is the fact that the pupil who is learning to post *with* the motion of his horse is, at the same time, learning a correct *jumping* position.

The rider who is in the correct position, enabling him to post with the motion, starts to acquire a good jumping position weeks before he sees a fence. There is no better exercise for getting and keeping a good jumping position than posting with the motion of your horse, because when you post with the motion, your hip angles open as little as necessary, your knee angles open and close, and your ankle angles stay closed. In jumping, we work with angles as one way of teaching riders how to be with a horse over a fence and at the same time not get ahead of him or push themselves so far out of the saddle in an effort to be with the horse that much of their security is lost. By studying the illustrations on this page, I think you will be able to see what I mean by these angles and get a pretty good idea of how they work.

The rider isn't asked to think about these angles while he is learning to post with the motion. The angles are automatically taken care of by adjusting the rider's position in the saddle. But he is learning to feel how these angles work so that by the time he is asked to think about them in the more advanced work, his co-ordination has become automatic. Meanwhile, by simply assuming the correct position in the saddle and working at the slow gaits first, your angles will begin to work automatically.

Another advantage of posting with the motion—especially for long rides or hunting—is the fact that much of the rider's weight is taken off the horse's back, giving him greater freedom of movement and making his work easier.

Posting with the motion also helps to overcome a more or less common tendency to get the legs too far out in front of the girth. When the rider's legs are too far in front of the girth, it is impossible for him to post with the motion. Learning to post with the motion brings the rider's legs into position, slightly behind the girth, where they not only contribute to the rider's security but also allow him the proper use of this important aid in controlling his horse.

Because it is so difficult for the beginner especially to learn and to keep the correct degree of forward inclination of the upper body when learning to post with the motion, we often see the novice tending to get ahead of his horse, or ahead of the motion. This happens when a rider gets out of the saddle too high and transfers his weight ahead of his points of support. Because he is out of balance, as the horse begins to move forward, he is thrown even farther forward so that he collapses on the horse's neck. When this happens, of course, much of the rider's security in the saddle is destroyed. It is, therefore, something for the beginner to be on guard against.

Much of this tendency on the part of the beginner to antici-

pate, or get ahead of his horse, can be overcome, if not eliminated entirely, by not being too anxious. *Learn to wait for your horse.*

Colonel Mariles, head of the famous Mexican Army Team, when approached by an admirer and asked for the secret of his incredibly smooth performances over fences, said, "The secret of good riding is—*wait for your horse. Feel* what your horse is going to do, and then—*wait for him!*"

Remember, it is the horse's job to throw you forward and upward, when posting with the motion. All *you* do is sink down in the saddle. The forward movement of the horse will then carry you back into position. Much of getting too far out of the saddle, twisting the upper body in mid-air before coming down, collapsing on the horse's neck, or, in the other extreme, being thrown too far back so that the legs shoot out in front of the rider, is caused by the rider's trying to do the horse's work for him. The horse throws you forward and upward. You sink down. The horse's forward motion carries you back. And until then—*Wait for him!*

Posting behind the motion, which should never be confused with posting *behind the horse,* is not only correct, but also sometimes essential to a good performance. When working with green horses, when working to put a horse on the bit, and when working with the *too-bold* horse, I post *behind* the motion. But for all other work, recommend that pupils post with the motion.

The rider who is learning to post with the motion, however, should *always* learn on a horse that is not too bold, or even a slightly sluggish one. In the early stages of learning to post with the motion, it is difficult for the rider not to have too much forward inclination of the upper body. This, of course, will urge a bold horse to be even bolder. For safety's sake, therefore, it is wiser to go to extremes, if necessary, in the other direction.

To summarize: a. Posting with the motion puts the pupil into the correct jumping position.

   b. It teaches him about opening and closing the knee angles that are so important to a smooth performance over fences.

   c. It enables all riders, of all degrees of riding skill, to look well on a horse and still feel secure.

Before closing this article on the posting trot, however, let me caution the over-enthusiastic beginner: Posting with the motion of the horse looks so smooth, and looks so easy, that you may be discouraged if you don't get it all at once, feeling that the fault is with you. But posting with the motion of the horse—and *not* ahead of the motion—cannot be learned overnight, and there are few riders who really post *with* the motion consistently.

Remember, too, that the rider's weight is carried in the heels. The ankles are flexed, as described in the foregoing chapter; a constant effort is made to depress the *heels:* and pressure is applied to and weight carried in the heels, *not* the stirrups.

LEARNING HOW TO POST WITH THE MOTION:

Learning to post with the motion does not require courage or skill, but it does take time. The rider needs a great deal of practice in the coordination of opening and closing the angles, and this should be learned at the standstill, with the rider rising and closing his kneed angles while slowly sinking in the saddle. Then, at the sitting trot, practice holding your upper body in the correct position and keeping the angle in your knees while the horse is in movement before attempting to post.

To assume the correct position for the posting trot, first *walk,* with the body inclined forward in a posting position. Then put the horse into a slow or sitting trot at six miles an hour. *Do not post.* As the horse trots, the rider should feel the crotch—and *not* the buttocks—hitting the saddle. *Now*—gradually—let the horse thrust you *forward* and slightly *upward,* then you sink downward and the impulsion of the horse carries you back. In rising to the trot, the angle at the hips should be opened as little as necessary. Opening the angle at the hips too much while posting to the trot causes the upper body to become almost vertical and causes a loss of balance as well as of security.

If the buttocks are in the saddle, you will find that your horse is throwing you upward and forward instead of forward and upward, and you will then be posting *behind* the motion.

Coming down, the rider must sink down in the saddle in order to post with the motion. With hip and knee angles closed, the rider makes no attempt to come back in the saddle as he comes down. The movement of the horse going forward will bring the rider back into position.

The rider should repeat this exercise for five minutes every time he rides to develop a secure jumping seat.

DIAGONALS: Before we leave the posting trot, we should learn a little bit about diagonals. Most people consider the correct diagonal important only in horsemanship events at horse shows, but everyone who rides in a riding hall should be able to tell whether or not he is posting on the correct diagonal.

When the rider sits down in the saddle each time the right forefoot strikes the ground, he is said to be posting on the right diagonal; when he sits down each time the left forefoot is planted, he is posting on the left diagonal. The rider should frequently alternate diagonals in order to insure equal development and power in the hind legs of the horse. On straight lines it is immaterial which diagonal the rider posts on, provided he uses both diagonals equally. But when working in a riding hall, a horse travels a great deal of the time on a curve. Therefore, his outside lateral travels a greater distance than his inside lateral; his outside hind leg travels further than his inside leg. In the ring, on the left hand, for example, the rider should post on the right diagonal, receiving the thrust of the left hind leg, which has the shorter distance to travel, and thus equalizing the work of the hind legs. The opposite, of course, is true when working on the right hand. In addition to equalizing the work of the horse's hind legs, being on the proper diagonal in a riding ring is an added safety factor when going around turns.

A quick and easy way to tell whether or not you are posting on the proper diagonal is to look down at your horse's shoulder. When you are in the saddle when your horse's right shoulder comes toward you, you are on the right diagonal. If the right shoulder is going away from you, you are on the left diagonal.

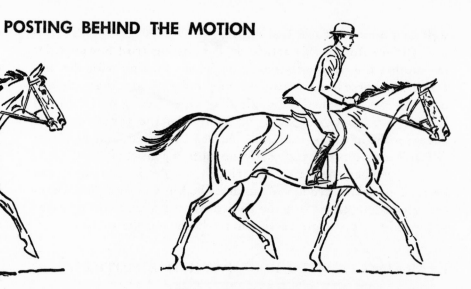

2. SPEED IS INCREASED TO THE SPEED OF THE POSTING TROT—8 Miles per hour. The rider is on the right diagonal, sitting down in the saddle as the horse's right fore foot strikes the ground.

3. The rider is thrust *upward* and *forward*, the hip angle remains the same, the knee angle opens. While the rider is in suspension, the horse's left fore foot strikes the ground.

1. THE RIDER GETS INTO POSITION AT THE SLOW OR SITTING TROT—6 Miles per hour, upper body vertical.

4. The rider now comes *backward* and *downward*, the hip angle opens, the knee angle closes slightly. This final movement of posting behind the motion is in sharp contrast with the similar movement in posting with the motion. Behind the motion, the rider comes back and down, two separate movements. With the motion, the rider merely sinks into his saddle, the forward motion of the horse carrying him back into position, which is one reason why posting with the motion tends to look like less "work" than posting behind the motion.

5. The rider is down in the saddle as the right forefoot once more strikes the ground.

POSTING WITH THE MOTION

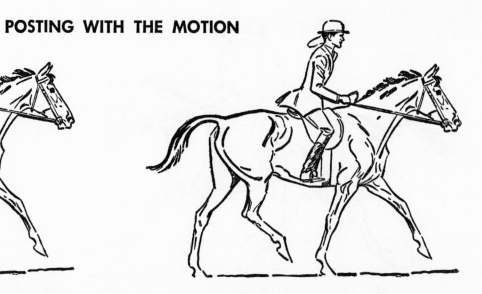

2. The rider's upper body inclines forward, *crotch* in the saddle, sitting the trot. It is impossible to post with the motion unless the crotch is touching the saddle.

3. The rider is sitting down as the horse's right forefoot strikes the ground.

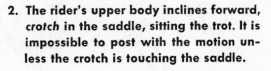

1. THE RIDER GETS INTO POSITION AT THE SLOW OR SITTING TROT—6 Miles per hour, upper body vertical.

4. The rider is thrust *forward* and *upward*.

5. The rider comes *downward* and the movement of the *horse carries him back*. The knee angles close. The hip angles open as little as necessary. The rider's *crotch* sinks into the saddle.

6. The rider is down in his saddle as the right forefoot once more strikes the ground.

Chapter VII

THE CANTER AND THE GALLOP

The Two-Point and the Three-Point Contact

When the horse is cantering, the rider should have a three-point contact. When the horse is galloping, the rider should have a two-point contact.

The rider has a three-point contact when his crotch is deep in the saddle, and the inner bones of the knees and the calves of the legs are all in contact with the horse.

The rider has a two-point contact when the inner bones of the knees and the calves of the legs are in contact with the saddle, and the crotch is *out* of the saddle. The rider's weight is carried in his heels, and this combination of legs and heels forms a vise-like grip on the horse which provides security for the rider even though he is out of the saddle.

At the canter, the rider should always have a three-point contact. He also has a three-point contact during his approach to the jump during the intermediate and advanced stages of jumping. He has a two-point contact at the gallop, with his weight entirely clear of the horse's back and the hindquarter, from which the horse derives all of his powers of propulsion, free to work without interference or hindrance from the rider.

At the canter, the horse moves at ten to twelve miles an hour; at the hand gallop, fourteen to sixteen miles an hour; and at the extended gallop, eighteen to twenty miles an hour.

As we have seen in the previous chapter, the horse moves at four miles an hour at the walk; six miles an hour at the slow trot; and eight miles an hour at the posting trot.

He moves at these speeds because he moves best at these speeds. A horse may be made to trot faster than eight miles an hour, but when he does trot faster than that, he is apt to have what is called a "disunited" trot, which means that his hind end is spraddled out, trying to catch up with his front end.

Similarly, allowing for conformation faults, these are the speeds at which a horse may safely be asked to canter or to gallop, and the speeds at which he can keep his hindquarters under him.

When jumping, the horse may be expected to jump a three-foot fence safely and well when he is going twelve miles an hour; a three-foot six at fourteen miles an hour; a four-foot at sixteen miles an hour. Very few horses jump safely when going faster than sixteen miles an hour.

A very common fault among people learning to jump is to "run the horse off his feet," especially at the lower fences. It is safe to say that more mistakes are made—both by the horse and by the rider—on the lower fences than on the higher fences. It's harder for the horse to judge his take-off; it's easier for the rider to "over-drive" or over-urge his horse riding down to the lower fences than when approaching the higher fences.

Speed is important. The horse must have enough propulsion to clear the fence. But he must not be over-ridden, therefore preventing him from getting his hindquarters under him.

If a horse has acquired the unfortunate habit of cross-cantering, try cantering him in small circles. The minute you feel him cross-cantering, circle him and keep him at the small circle until he has corrected himself. Then take him back out on the track, repeating the circle again the minute you feel his hind-quarters taking the wrong lead. This is no sure cure for this annoying habit, but it sometimes produces results, especially if the rider is also careful to put the horse onto his lead from the slow or sitting trot collecting him first as described in this chapter, and not letting him roll into it.

A CORRECT POSITION AT THE CANTER

The rider is using a Three-Point Contact, with the crotch deep in the saddle, the inner bones of the knees and the calves of the legs coming into contact with the saddle.

A CORRECT GALLOPING POSITION

The rider is using a Two-Point Contact, which consists of the inner bones of the knees and the lower part of the legs, the weight carried in the *heels* not the stirrups.

PART III

Chapter I

THE ADVANCED AIDS

In an earlier chapter, you have learned about the elementary aids and how they work on a horse: primarily to ask for and to control the increase and decrease of forward motion. But before going on to the more advanced phases of jumping and riding, the rider should be able to understand, and to apply, some of the more advanced aids. It should always be borne in mind that whether we are discussing the use of the aids, or controls, in their most elementary form, or in the most advanced form (which you will come to in a later chapter of this book), we are always using the same aids, although we are using them in different and sometimes more complicated ways, to achieve different and more complicated results.

There are two kinds of aids, which we speak of as natural aids and artificial aids. The natural aids are:

The reins,

The legs,

The weight, and occasionally,

The voice.

The artificial aids are:

The spur,

The whip or riding bat,

A variety of bits.

Before any of these aids can be applied effectively, the horse must be put on the bit. *To put the horse on the bit:*

As soon as the rider has picked up his reins and, with the aid of leg pressure, established contact with his horse's mouth, the horse—in a very simple and elementary way—has been put "on the bit." The horse is on the bit when he willingly has moved up to accept the pressure of the bit in his mouth. This pressure is light at the slow gaits, and becomes quite frank at the faster gaits as the horse leans on the bit more and more. It is this leaning on the bit on the part of the horse that makes it possible for the rider to decrease the horse's speed simply by taking a feel and holding it, refusing to yield until the horse has broken and come down to the required gait. The weight of the horse *against* the bit as he attempts to move faster is certainly greater than any pressure which could be applied by the rider against the bit, through hauling on the reins.

A horse is said to be "nicely on the bit" when he flexes his poll, brings his chin in, and puts his weight on the rider's hands where it may be controlled.

A horse that is behind the bit, or one who refuses to accept the bit, is a difficult horse to ride and a tricky horse to jump. A horse signals his intention of running out by dropping—or trying to drop—his head. If he is on the bit, the rider feels that immediately, and takes steps to avoid it. But the horse who is behind the bit can run out at will.

There is a right way and a wrong way of putting the horse on the bit, a good way and a bad way.

For the beginner, picking up the reins, as I said before, and applying a slight pressure of the legs will "put the horse on the bit," because training and schooling have already taught him to accept the bit and move up into it.

Young horses and green horses, and some particularly light-mouthed horses are behind the bit. The young horse's training should be slow enough so that he can be properly put on the bit before attempting to jump him. Time spent properly putting the horse on the bit while he is young or green will reward the rider a thousandfold in safety and good performances.

It is difficult to ride a horse that is not on the bit, and I don't recommend it for the rider who is just learning the use of his controls.

CORRECT USE OF THE ADVANCED AIDS
The Reins

The reins are the first aid which the rider is called upon to use, and it is important to know that there are five different rein actions, each producing a different effect.

A direct rein: Is what the rider uses, as we have already seen, to increase and decrease speed. It is also used for backing and for turning. It is called a "direct" rein because of the direct line it makes from the horse's mouth to the rider's elbow. It displaces weight from the forehand to the haunches and it is the rein most frequently used for all riding, hunting, and showing.

An indirect rein: It displaces weight laterally from one side to the other and is used to put a horse into a canter, and also for making some turns.

A leading rein: It displaces weight in the direction of movement and is used to turn the horse in any direction and is especially useful with young or green horses, since it acts in a very simple way.

A bearing or neck rein: Used primarily on polo ponies, or at any time when the rider wishes to change direction without noticeably decreasing the speed. The reins are held in one hand, as illustrated here.

A pulley rein: Which is a very powerful rein effect. It works like a pulley and is used, as a rule, only when it is necessary to make a very sudden stop. The left hand is set, or fixed slightly in front of the horse's withers while the right hand acts to draw the right rein to the rear of the horse's withers and to the side which is in opposition to the side on which the rider's hand is fixed. Used sharply, either with or without the aid of the leg, this has the effect of overbalancing the horse very suddenly to one side and, therefore, bringing him down to an abrupt halt.

The leg as an aid works in two ways; it is either active or passive. The legs should only be active when the rider desires to increase the horse's motion, either moving him directly ahead or to either side. Both legs become active to move the horse forward. For other movements which require the horse's impulsion, the legs may act either together or one at a time. When impulsion is not required, the leg should be passive. If one leg works to move the horse to the side or move his haunches to the right or to the left, the passive leg does not come into action unless the horse decreases the speed at which he is moving. Then the passive leg "oversees" the action of the active leg, so that the proper degree of propulsion is produced and continued.

If the rider is squeezing his horse, his legs are active. If, through insecurity in the saddle, the rider is unable to keep his leg still against the horse's sides, his leg is an active leg. If he squeezes his horse either for security or out of a nervous apprehension, his leg is *active*.

Any, or all, of these forms of an active leg are conflicting with the rider's hands against his horse's mouth, or causing the rider to clash his controls, if the hands increase pressure on the horse's mouth to decrease the speed which the intentionally or unintentionally active leg has produced.

There is an INSIDE LEG on a horse and an OUTSIDE LEG. The rider's inside leg is the leg on the inside of a turn or partial turn. The rider's outside leg is the leg on the outside of a turn or partial turn.

When a movement calls for the use of only one leg at a time, care must be exercised to see that the other leg is really passive, to avoid clashing the controls.

The use of the aids for the increase and decrease of speed has already been explained in the chapter, "Elementary Aids." Now, however, the rider should have spent a sufficient number of hours in the saddle so that he is able to use his artificial aids to produce impulsion if the natural aid—the leg—proves insufficient.

Spurs, needless to say, should not be used indiscriminately on any horse. But when you know your horse and know how he responds, and if he needs the use of the spur because of a sluggish disposition or a side that has become sour to the leg, then the spur may be used to increase speed when the pressure of the legs closing about the horse has failed to produce the necessary impulsion.

If the spur doesn't work, then the riding bat is used. To use a riding bat correctly make a bridge of the reins, and hold them in one hand, with the bight—or extra rein—on the side *opposite* the side on which the bat is to be used or applied. When the horse has been struck *lightly* on the flank—since it is the noise of a feathered bat rather than the force of it which will generally give us all the forward impulsion we need or want—the rider's hand comes immediately back to his reins, where it once more continues its job of controlling the horse. In using a bat the arm pivots at the shoulder but the rest of the body must not move.

To decrease speed, the rider's hands close on the reins and hold that feel until the horse has responded by coming down to the required gait. If closing the hands is not enough—and it very often is not, under the special emergency conditions of, say, the hunt field—then the rider immediately resorts to the use of the pulley rein, which *no* horse can resist if the rider's hand is firmly set, and even pressed, against the horse's withers for support while using the opposite hand to bring him back and throw him off balance to one side.

Circling for the decrease of speed is something used often and with great success in slowing a horse down between fences. To be successful, however, the rider must continue to circle until the horse is completely relaxed. The minute he shows signs of rushing toward his fence again, he is once more turned sharply away and circled just before and in front of the jump, the circle coming closer and closer to the jump until the rider feels the horse has relaxed sufficiently to take the jump.

Circling is good for a bold horse, too. If, when you first get on a horse, he's feeling too "high" for you, try to work him in a ring around a fence or other object, starting with a quite small circle and gradually making the circle wider and wider. A horse's mentality is, fortunately for the rider, somewhat limited. When we put his mind on something else—like keeping his balance at a circle—he soon takes it off his original intent—to play and buck.

The same method of disciplining and the same use of the aids can be made to work with the horse that attempts to rear, kick out, or resist in place. By using the aids to move the horse *forward,* keeping a firm though light contact with his mouth, the rider can get him out of his original disobedience and take steps later to see that it is not repeated.

THE COORDINATION OF THE AIDS: The aids are coordinated when one aid is used to follow up or to assist the effect of another aid. It is extremely important for the rider to remember that he must use only one aid at a time. In the hands of the skilled horseman, the aids are applied so deftly that it seems as though they are being used simultaneously. But because the aids are signals to the horse, and sometimes very strong signals, they should be used one at a time, although, of course, they may and sometimes should follow one another very closely, as in the case of using the aids to put the horse into a canter.

DIAGONAL AND LATERAL AIDS: Just as there are two kinds

of aids, natural and artificial, just so there are two ways in which these aids may be used—diagonally and laterally. Lateral aids are aids that work on one side of a horse at a time; diagonal aids are aids that work on both sides. A right rein, or a right rein and a right leg, are lateral aids. A right rein and a left leg, working together, would be a diagonal aid.

When putting a horse into a canter, the diagonal aids are used. The rider applies the right indirect rein in front of the withers, displacing the weight from the right shoulder to the left, leaving the horse's right foreleg free to move. Then the rider's left leg becomes active, transferring the horse's weight from the left hind to the right hind. The rider's left leg then acts to produce the extra impulsion that puts the horse into a canter.

USE OF THE AIDS WHEN MAKING A TURN: When the right hand closes on the rein in making a turn, the left hand must become passive. When the left hand closes, the right hand becomes passive.

USE OF THE WEIGHT AS AN AID: The rider's weight as an aid may usually be counted upon to work automatically if the rider's eyes are up and focused in the direction in which he is going or in which he intends to go. The eyes, to a great extent, influence and direct the balance of the upper body in the saddle, so that just looking where you want to go is usually better than trying to shift your weight. For the beginner, especially, a conscious effort to shift the weight when making a turn toward a jump will all too often result in an exaggeration which causes the horse to overturn.

The opening of the hip angles also acts to distribute the rider's weight farther back in the saddle, and is used as an aid in decreasing the gait. Conversely, closing the hip angle and increasing the forward inclination of the upper body acts as an aid in increasing the gait.

USE OF THE VOICE AS AN AID: The voice can sometimes be an important aid, especially for the rider when, through insecurity, lack of experience, or faulty conformation, he is not able to make proper use of the leg aid. Rather than run the risk of having such a rider squeeze his horse when the legs should be passive, or kick himself out of the saddle, quite literally, in attempting to use the legs to produce impulsion, I recommend the use of the voice with some other aid or control.

To produce impulsion at the jump by use of the voice, I have the rider hold his horse at a standstill and use a bat, striking the horse lightly on the flank and clucking at the same time. Because the horse associates the sound of the voice with the feel of the bat, the rider has only to cluck to his horse, and the horse will move forward exactly as though the rider had used a bat.

The voice can be used effectively to help decrease the speed if the rider will spend a few minutes applying pressure on the reins and at the same time use his voice to say, "who-a" sharply and firmly. The horse will gradually learn to respond to the voice with very little or no feel on the reins. This is useful at a show when riding a course of jumps and wishing a slight decrease of speed without noticeable tension on the reins.

TO LEARN THE CORRECT COORDINATION OF THE AIDS: The rider moves the horse forward, his eyes up and focused in the direction in which he intends to travel. As the horse moves into the required gait, the eyes stay up, resisting the tendency to look down at the horse. As the rider begins to apply his different aid, he should be made to feel how much pressure should be used, depending upon the horse. In this, as in all phases of riding, the rider should be cautioned to make haste slowly. First, a gentle pressure of the legs is applied to the horse's side as the rider asks for an increase of speed, and not until that fails to produce results are other aids used.

The rider should learn the use and coordination of the aids by moving from the standstill to the walk, to the slow trot, then back to the halt. This teaches the rider the use of his various aids while applying them slowly, one at a time, until their coordination has become more or less automatic and the rider has developed a feel of how the horse responds.

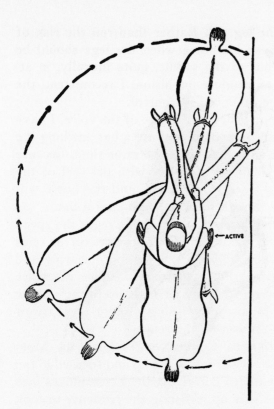

THIS IS A TURN ON THE FOREHAND

1. The direct rein and active legs put the horse on the bit.

2. The left indirect rein in front of the withers displaces the weight from the left fore to the right fore, forcing that to become the pivot for the turn.

3. An active right leg turns the horse, displacing the haunches from right to left.

4. The passive left leg becomes active if the horse attempts to back from the rein action.

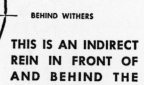

← IN FRONT OF WITHERS

← BEHIND WITHERS

THIS IS AN INDIRECT REIN IN FRONT OF AND BEHIND THE WITHERS

The Indirect Rein in front of the withers is used to make the turn on the forehand, the turn on the haunches, and the canter departure. The Indirect Rein behind the withers is used for the shoulder-in, for bending, and for two-tracking.

THIS IS A TURN ON THE HAUNCHES

1. The direct rein and active legs put the horse on the bit. **2.** The left indirect rein in front of the withers works together with a left active leg. **3.** The right direct rein and the right passive leg assist the left indirect rein to make the turn on the haunches. **4.** The right passive leg becomes active if the horse attempts to back up from the rein action.

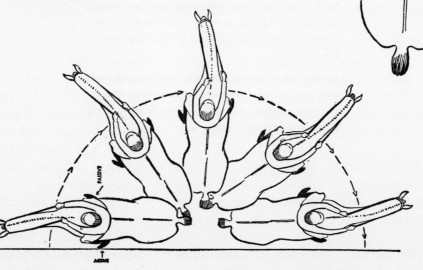

79

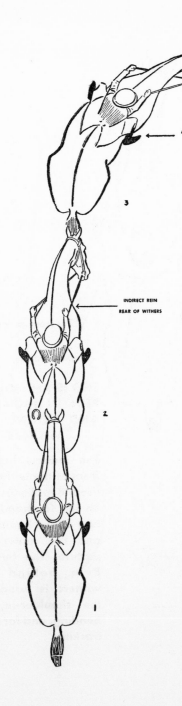

ACTIVE LEG

3

INDIRECT REIN
REAR OF WITHERS

2

1

HOW TO TURN, OR "BEND" YOUR HORSE

This is the correct way to turn, or, "bend," your horse when working in a ring.

1. Shows the rider looking into the corner and riding with a direct rein.

2. The rider is looking into the opposite corner and applying an indirect rein in front of the withers.

3. At the turn, the rider applies an active leg with the indirect rein, to make the horse bend in the corner, fitting into the corner like a bow.

In the last two movements, the rider's eyes are focused on the opposite corner. This is the way a horse should *always* be turned in a ring or riding hall.

THE BEARING REIN

Displaces weight from one side to the other. It is used for polo ponies, stock horses, or any time a sudden turn is required without a noticeable decrease in speed. The illustration above shows a polo player using the bearing rein for a turn. Notice the player's eyes focused in the direction he intends to go, and the pony being brought back on his haunches to make the turn.

A PULLEY REIN

This is a very powerful rein effect. It works like a pulley and is used, as a rule, only when it is necessary to make a very sudden stop. The left hand is set, or fixed, on the horse's wither, while the other hand acts to draw the rein to the rear of the horse's wither and to the side which is in opposition to the side on which the rider's hand is fixed. Used sharply, either with or without the aid of the leg, this has the effect of over-balancing the horse very suddenly to one side and, therefore, bringing him down to an abrupt halt.

THIS IS A LEADING REIN

It displaces weight in the direction of movement. Its effect and use is to turn the horse to the right from any direction. It is particularly useful when working with very young or green horses since its action is a simple one.

THIS IS A DIRECT REIN

It makes a direct line from horse's mouth to rider's elbow. It is used to control forward motion and to distribute the horse's weight from forehand to haunches. It is the rein which is used mostly in all riding, hunting and showing.

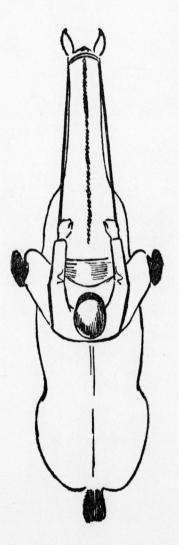

Chapter II

SCHOOLING MOVEMENTS

Their Purpose and Their Importance

Schooling movements are limbering exercises for your horse. They are important to him, and he should do them fairly regularly for the same reason that human beings should have regular exercise: they keep him fit and in condition.

Schooling movements serve another important purpose: They act as a constant reminder and refresher course in the use, application and coordination of the aids.

To be effective, any schooling movement that is used should be one that utilizes a horse's shoulder and neck muscles. Schooling movements should also be planned so that they teach the horse responsiveness to the rein and leg aids, and instill in him the habit of obedience to the rider's commands.

Any rider will find that the time spent learning and practicing the schooling movements which are described and illustrated in this chapter is time well spent. Many a hunter or jumper class has been lost because the horse was allowed to turn too soon, or cut a corner sharply and approach the fence from an awkward or, a disadvantageous angle. There isn't time, when riding in a show, or in the hunt field, for the rider consciously to think about which leg or rein aid to use in turning his horse. Schooling movements, conscientiously practiced, will make these reactions on the part of the rider automatic, so that when he is riding a course of jumps all he will have on his mind is all that he *should* have on his mind—

Keeping his pace, and keeping his eyes up, looking in the direction in which he intends to move.

All of the following schooling movements call for the use of the different aids, applied either individually, in sequence, or simultaneously. Any, or all of them, are fine exercises for both horse and rider, particularly when working in the ring and limbering up before taking a course of jumps. It is never a good idea just to work a horse around in a circle. He should be kept limber and alert by asking him to perform such simple exercises as these, which will help make and keep him a better athlete and, therefore, a better jumper.

RECOMMENDED SCHOOLING MOVEMENTS
Trotting and Stopping

An excellent exercise to teach the rider coordination of the aids in stopping his horse, and to help "mouth" a young, green, or badly-mouthed horse. The rider trots a third of the way around the ring, say, then applies his direct rein aid, keeping his eyes up, and closing his hands on the reins, applying and holding pressure until the horse comes to a standstill. Relax hands for reward. He keeps the horse at the standstill to the count of five, then puts the horse into forward motion once more, from the walk to the slow trot to the posting trot. Another third of the way around the ring, the hands again close on the reins, pressure is applied until the horse comes once more to a standstill, and again the rider mentally counts to five. Then the horse is again moved forward, and so on, gradually increasing the time and the distance between halts as the horse reacts by flexing his poll and showing that he is responding to training by coming back with less pressure applied on his mouth each time. At the end of ten minutes or so, the horse should be responding easily to the use of the reins, and requiring very little pressure against his mouth.

When trotting and stopping a horse, the things to remember in order to make the exercise effective for both horse and rider:

Be sure the horse is stopped *in a straight line*. Don't let him swing his hindquarters out into the ring. If he does, use the inside leg and inside rein to bring him back into line again. It is important for horses to learn to stop in a straight line. It makes them much better company on a hunt or even when just out hacking in company.

When the horse has come down to a standstill, be sure that it *is* a standstill. The rider's hands should relax their pressure the instant the horse has come to a standstill, but pressure is immediately applied again if the horse attempts to walk forward. A standstill means a standstill, not moving in place, turning this way or that. Like all schooling movements, the thoroughness with which these easy things are done can mean much to the comfort and safety of the rider later on.

And be very, *very* sure that your hands relax the instant the horse has flexed his poll and obeyed your command by coming to a standstill. The rider's hands should be completely relaxed while he is mentally counting to five, with the horse at a standstill. It helps, while standing still, to stroke the horse. Stroking may or may not relax the horse, but it is certain to relax the rider, and a relaxed rider usually means a relaxed horse.

Don't keep at this or any other schooling exercise for too long at a time. Remember that the horse's intelligence is a limited one. Most horses do not learn easily. Schooling exercises—even the simplest ones—impose a severe strain on the horse as he tries to understand what is wanted of him and to yield to the command. Therefore, ten minutes of any schooling exercise is enough. Then let the horse completely relax on a loose rein.

When it is continued for too long at a time, trotting and stopping, like any schooling exercise, will tend to make a horse sour and disobedient because of the strain that is imposed on him. But it is an exercise which I recommend most highly for the rider who has trouble making his horse come back to him on proper application of the rein aids. In an elementary way, it helps teach the horse to flex his poll, and by forcing him to stand still while other horses in the ring move past him, it discourages the bad habit which so many horses have, of darting forward to keep up with the horse ahead of them.

Trotting and stopping is good for the horse who tends to hang in the rider's hands, or shows any other tendency to resist pressure on the reins. It is a slow, safe, easy way to teach a horse to respond to the rider's controls, and to teach the rider to use those controls gently and correctly.

THE CIRCLE

The rider being on the track, at the walk, slow trot, trot, or canter, describes a complete circle parallel to the track and retakes the track at the point where he left it. (See Illustration.)

THE CIRCLE

The diameter of the circle at the walk — 1 yard
At the slow or sitting trot — 2 yards
At the posting trot — 3 yards
At the canter — 4 yards

THE FIGURE EIGHT

This exercise consists of describing the figure of eight first at the walk, the slow trot, the posting trot, and, finally, the canter, with a change of leads in the middle of the figure. At the trot, the rider changes his diagonals. At the canter, he first comes down to a slow trot for a step or two before taking his horse into the canter departure on the opposite lead. This assures that the horse is collected, with his hindquarters properly engaged under him, allowing him to take the lead from the hindquarters rather than roll into it from the forehand and run the risk of having him cross-canter. Later on, of course, when the rider's controls are working smoothly, the figure eight may be cantered, with a flying change of the lead.

FIGURE OF EIGHT

When making the figure eight, note that *both* sides are equal in diameter.

SERPENTINE

Consists of successive abouts, executed as illustrated. Again the diameter is the same as that of the circle. In other words, trotting the serpentine, the rider will have a longer parallel line and a wider circle at the end of each line than if he were cantering the serpentine. The diameter changes with the different gaits, as listed above, but *not* with the different movements.

When making the serpentine at the trot, the rider changes his diagonals. At the canter, he has the choice of keeping his horse on a false lead, or changing leads, which amounts to a flying change of the lead or breaking back to a trot and then putting the horse on the correct lead. The flying change of the lead is something I do not recommend to the rider whose aids are not working very smoothly. To attempt the flying change of the lead before the aids can be used in swift and easy coordination with one another is to run the risk of developing a "mouth" problem and a horse who learns to reach and bore as he attempts to escape the strong use of the rider's legs before the rider has learned to relax his hands at the same time.

THE HALF TURN

Consists of an about followed by an oblique. (See Illustration.)

Being on the track on the left hand, at the walk, slow trot or trot, the rider describes a left about and then by the left oblique regains the track.

At the moment the horse starts the left about, the rider, by applying the right indirect rein in front of the withers and an active right leg, turns the horse on his haunches.

This movement is an excellent exercise for learning and perfecting the turn on the haunches.

THE HALF TURN

This is a half-turn. The diameter of the half-turn is the same as that of the full circle.

THE HALF TURN IN REVERSE

An oblique followed by an about. (See Illustration.)

Being on the track on the left hand, at the walk or slow trot, the rider turns to the left oblique and then, at the proper time, by a right about regains the track.

At the moment the horse starts the right about the rider, by increasing the action of the left leg and left indirect rein, has caused the horse to turn on the haunches.

This is a particularly fine exercise for teaching the rider to keep his eyes up.

WHEN RIDING IN A RING OR RIDING HALL: The rider can work constantly to improve his seat, his balance in the saddle, his control over his horse and his general horsemanship if:

At the trot, the diagonal should be changed as and when the direction is changed.

When working a bold, or high-feeling horse, always circle, unless, of course, the horse is suffering or recovering from some kind of lameness, in which case all circling and rotating should be avoided. Circling a horse takes his mind off his ideas of playing by putting it on the problem of keeping himself in proper balance while circling. For this reason, start with a very small circle, or circle around a standard, or a barrel, and then gradually, as you feel the horse relaxing under you, widen the circle to take in half a ring and then, finally, a full ring.

When beginning to work a horse over jumps in a ring, jump *away* from the outgate or stable for the first few jumps until the horse has settled down. A horse will always tend to rush his fences at first, and this tendency is sharply increased, especially at the beginning of the lesson, if he is jumped toward the stable. By working first away from the stable and then toward it, the horse will settle down to his work much more quickly and with much less pressure on his mouth or on the reins.

If a horse shows a tendency to run after taking a jump, and especially if his mouth is on the hard or difficult side, I recommend the use of the wall to stop him rather than the reins. By this I mean, head the horse directly toward the wall when he has finished his jump, letting him bump his nose a few times if necessary. It will soon teach him to slow down on the other side, and save his mouth from the severe punishment which would otherwise be necessary.

Another excellent schooling exercise for making an athlete of your horse is the use of successive, multiple in-and-outs, all set very low. This is an exercise which you will find described in detail in the section devoted to jumping.

Chapter III

ELEMENTARY JUMPING

This first stage, or phase, of learning to jump is something which the beginner may learn at the same time that he is learning the posting trot. As I explained back in the chapter on "Position," everything the rider does, and everything he learns in assuming this position on a horse, is fitting him for the jumping, showing, and hunting which he will do as soon as his seat in the saddle has become secure and he has learned the meaning and importance of a line of sight. To get and keep a line of sight, the rider should not only have learned to keep his eye up but also to keep them focused on one special point or object. The best way to acquire the habit of keeping a line of sight is for the instructor to stand in front of the jump, reminding the pupil to keep his eyes focused on the instructor.

There is no magic formula for learning how to jump, and looking well while you are learning. I have said before, and I will say again, that jumping, even the quite high jumps, up to four foot six or so—does *not* take nerve, or special physical attributes, or any exceptional athletic skill or ability. It takes only one thing, and that one thing is—*confidence.*

Now that the rider is about to learn how to assume a jumping position and to hold it over his first jump—either a real or imaginary rail on the ground—it is time for him to realize that all of his future work, and the rapidity with which progress can and will be made, depends entirely upon his developing confidence. First, confidence in his instructor. He must believe in his instructor sufficiently to do what he is told to do without question and without reservation—even a mental question or a mental reservation. If the pupil cannot have this complete and absolute confidence in his instructor, then he is wasting the money he is spending on riding lessons.

When people are just learning how to ride, they very often are over-mounted, which may shake their confidence or finish them with riding for good. But a great deal of the time, they find themselves over-mounted because of some false pride which keeps them from admitting (to the riding instructor or their friends) how little they do ride, or, more important, how hesitant or timid they really feel.

For the benefit of all these would-be and about-to-be riders, let me say that everyone is hesitant and timid about some horses and some kinds of riding or jumping, no matter how courageous a rider he may be. Because courage can only come from confidence, anyone who has had a bad experience on a horse will lose his confidence and, therefore, his nerve, temporarily. But if he has been taught what to do, and if he knows why the accident happened, his confidence can always be restored.

Therefore, don't hurry this early work. I have said it before, I know, but I must say it again, because all the rider's future confidence and enjoyment on a horse are at stake. Setbacks in the early stages of learning how to ride are much worse than the setbacks that come later, when the rider knows the special risk he has taken, or the more dangerous horse he has ridden because he wanted to ride him. In these early stages, the rider must have only good experience. He should not fall off; he should never have the experience or the feeling of a horse out of control; he should finish each lesson, or each day's work, with a good feeling, looking forward with real enjoyment, and not with an agony of apprehension, to the lesson to follow.

ELEMENTARY JUMPING
First Stage

The rider may begin to learn how to jump at the same time that he is learning the posting trot, his first jumping lesson to begin after the rider has put in ten to twenty hours in the saddle.

1. The rider is trotting around the ring at the slow, or six-mile-an-hour trot in a jumping position, maintaining a three-point contact which consists of: the crotch deeply in the saddle; the inner bones of the knees and the calves of the legs against the horse's sides; and the upper body inclined forward.

2. Before approaching the jump—which is either a rail on the ground or an *imaginary* rail on the ground—he moves his hands halfway up the horse's crest, preferably using the mane to steady himself, and putting the weight of the upper body on his hands and on the horse's neck.

3. He then rises out of his saddle, maintaining a *two-point* contact of the inside of the inner bones of the knees, and the calves of the legs against the horse's sides. The weight of the base and of the legs goes into the rider's heels—*not the stirrups.*

4. The rider keeps this position, whether the horse actually makes a little hopping jump over the rail on the ground or whether he merely trots over it. It is not an exercise in jumping; it is an exercise in learning to take and to hold the proper jumping position. For this reason, the rider should practice this stage of elementary jumping for quite some time—measured by riding hours, of course—before attempting to move into the second stage of elementary jumping, which brings him to cross-rails, where the horse will definitely make a jump and give the rider the feeling of a jump.

THE THINGS TO AVOID: When learning the posting trot, you are cautioned against trying to do the horse's work for him. In learning to post with the motion, the rider waits, lets the horse thrust him forward and *upward*. He comes down, and the forward motion of the horse carries him back.

In learning how to jump, the same principle holds true, only it is harder to learn and harder still to practice.

From the time the rider is learning to trot over his very first rail on the ground, he must start to learn that all-important and fundamental principle of successful, and, therefore, safe jumping: wait for your horse. The rider takes his position, as I have described above, and holds it, whether the horse jumps or not. He does not anticipate the jump. The rider, in other words, does not "jump" any more than the rider pulls himself up out of the saddle when he is learning to post.

In posting, the horse throws you up, you sink down and his forward motion carries you back. In jumping, the upward thrust of the horse's forehand clearing the fence throws the rider forward, and all the rider should do is to take his correct position and *hold* it. The horse will do the rest. In this phase of jumping, you are already up so the horse doesn't thrust you.

To make a conscious effort to jump when you think the horse is—or isn't—going to jump, puts the rider *ahead* of his horse, not *with* his horse. When the rider is ahead of the horse, he has lost much of his security and most of his control over his horse.

Obviously, while the rider is in this stage of elementary jumping, his instructor must see to it that he has a horse that requires little or no control and is quiet and obedient. The rider must have nothing on his mind but the job of learning to keep his eyes on a point, to move his hands forward, taking his correct jumping position and holding it.

Time spent practicing this movement on a horse will be time well spent, because the rider who can learn to move his hands for-ward automatically, under any and all jumping conditions; to keep his eyes up and feel what his horse is going to do instead of guessing or anticipating, is on the way to being a rider with a secure, safe, and smooth jumping position on *any height fence*.

THE FIRST STAGE OF ELEMENTARY JUMPING

The rider's hands are halfway up the horse's crest, the weight of the rider's upper body is on the rider's hands and the horse's crest. The rider stands up in the stirrups, maintaining a two-point contact of the inner bones of the knees and the calves of the legs in light contact with the horse's sides. The weight of the rider's legs and base goes to the rider's depressed heels and *not to the stirrups!*

ELEMENTARY JUMPING
Second Stage

In this second stage of elementary jumping, the rider does exactly the same things which he has practiced doing in the first stage of elementary jumping. His hands move forward, his eyes are up, he rises out of the saddle with a two-point contact. The only difference is that now the rider is going over a cross-rail and the horse actually jumps, giving the rider the feeling of a jump and making it slightly more difficult, but just as important, to keep his position.

ELEMENTARY JUMPING
Third Stage

In the third, and final stage of elementary jumping, the rider is cantering toward the jump whereas, in the first two stages, the rider was in a trot going toward the jump. As you will see, this series is planned so that first the rider learns to assume his correct jumping position trotting over a real or imaginary rail on the ground and being put under no nervous strain or tension whatsoever. If the rider is apprehensive about the size fence he is about to jump, a good rule of thumb to follow is, he shouldn't be jumping that size fence! Horses don't like to jump. They are quick to sense any slightest hesitancy on the part of the rider, and the horse quickly loses his own heart, or confidence.

Therefore, to recapitulate before we learn this last stage of elementary jumping: the rider is asked to assume and learn his jumping position while trotting over a rail on the ground so as to eliminate entirely any tenseness, fear, or apprehension and put the rider's mind where it should be at this stage of learning to jump— on assuming a correct jumping position.

The rider is kept at the slow gait, namely the trot, while he begins to accustom his body angles to the slight shock of jumping a cross-rail and getting the actual feel of a jump.

I am sure it is not necessary to say that while the rider is going through these early stages of learning how to jump, HE MUST BE MOUNTED ON SAFE, QUIET, STEADY HORSES. The rider should not be asked to think about controlling his horse until some security over even a very low jump has been achieved.

He now begins to get not only the feeling of a jump, but also the feeling of speed going into the jump. The speed, at this stage, is still controlled and should be approximately 12 miles per hour. Of course, the rider is still on a horse that has to be urged rather than one that has to be held. But he is now asked to put his horse into a canter which is a three-point contact. Approximately 20 yards away from the jump he assumes his two-point contact in the saddle, precisely as he did at the posting trot. He holds that position of the two-point contact until the horse has cleared the jump, and then sinks into a three-point contact again, for the canter. *Exercises:* A horse in fair condition can take this cross-rail jump approximately 100 times in an hour.

For the first exercise, the rider concentrates on keeping his eyes on some point directly ahead. The exercise consists of keeping the eyes on that point and then concentrating on keeping the weight of the upper body and the hands on the horse's crest. If instead of pushing, the hands pull, it is wrong. I recommend the use of the mane in these extremely early stages because there is nothing more harmful to both horse and rider than to run the risk of having the rider's hands come back, thus souring and interfering with the horse.

Keep at this exercise until hands push down on the crest for at least ten consecutive jumps.

In the second exercise, the rider concentrates on his heels. The weight of the base and the legs goes into the heels; the foot rests on the stirrup; and as little weight as possible goes into the stirrup. By letting weight sink into the heels you form a vise with your legs, which is the foundation of a sound, secure seat.

For the next step, repeat exercise 1, 2, and 3, ten times each, concentrating only on one point at a time.

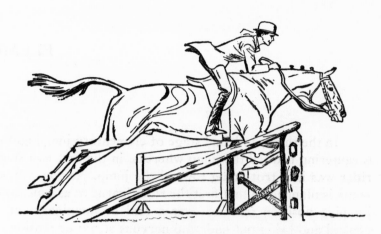

2. The approach: An average distance of from five to twenty yards away from the jump. a) Eyes are on a point. b) The hands move halfway up the horse's crest, or mane. The rider places the weight of the upper body on the hands and crest. c) The weight of legs and base goes into the rider's heels and not the stirrups. Contact is maintained through the inner bones of the knees and the calves of the legs, in light contact against the horse's sides. The rider rises out of the saddle with a two-point contact.

3. Take-off: The rider holds this position, and the thrust of the horse throws him forward. The rider doesn't "jump." He waits and, as the horse jumps, the rider is thrown forward and upward by the thrust of the horse.

The hip angles close, the knee angles remain open.

1. In the third stage of elementary jumping, the rider is permitted to canter into a cross rail, which means a three-point contact. The rider is in a three-point contact, cantering toward the jump.

4. The flight. The rider holds his position.

5. The landing. The hip angles open, knee angles close, the rider starts to *sink* down—not *sit* down—in the saddle, the flexed-in ankles and inner bones of knees acting to absorb shock of landing.

ELEMENTARY JUMPING
(Third Stage)

6. The rider resumes contact with the horse's mouth and continues the canter in the three-point contact.

Chapter IV

INTERMEDIATE JUMPING

The biggest difference between intermediate and elementary jumping is that now the rider, approaching the jump, will not assume the two-point contact himself, but will wait for the horse, taking off, to throw him up into the two-point contact. The rider has more feel of his horse, greater use of his legs, and greater control with the three-point contact than he can have with the two-point contact. There is, however, an obvious danger and an obvious disadvantage to the rider's attempting to use the three-point contact before his seat is sufficiently secure so that his hands are able to work independently of his body. When the rider begins to ride toward the jump with a three-point contact, there is infinitely more danger of his being left. This, in itself, is not so great a crime. The crime lies in the rider jabbing his horse severely in the mouth because he lacks the timing, physical control over his body, and independent use of his hands necessary to "get with his horse" in mid-air, or at least to thrust his hands forward, even if his seat is left, and thus avoid punishing the horse's mouth.

Until the rider's hands are acting independently of his body, he should jump with a two-point contact. When the hands *can* move forward automatically and work independently of the rider's body, then the three-point contact gives him, as I say, greater security and greater use of the leg aid.

And remember again, to KEEP YOUR EYES UP, focused on some definite point or object within the range of vision.

EXERCISE FOR LEARNING TO HOLD YOUR POSITION: Start with an in-and-out at two feet, coming into the first jump with a three-point contact. The horse thrusts you into a two-point contact. Keep this position over the next jump.

NOW: Holding that position, have the number of jumps increased. You start with a regulation in-and-out at two feet. You add a third two-foot fence. The distance between the jumps is eight feet. Gradually adding to these, you build up to six or seven or even eight, two-foot fences, eight feet apart. When the horse and rider have learned to negotiate these safely, the distance between jumps may be varied, so that the first two are eight feet apart, the third ten, the fourth eight, and so on.

The rewards of this exercise are obvious: The rider learns, first, to keep his hands up. Then, he learns to *feel* his horse, so that his hands will go up at the right time. In addition, the horse is taught to gauge his stride, measure his fences, and become alert as well as athletic. In the beginning, the rider will find even the most seasoned horse making a mistake over these fences as the distance between fences is altered and alternated. But with time and practice, both horse and rider will learn an athletic co-ordination.

2. At the approach, the rider's hands move up half-way on the horse's crest, the weight of the upper body and the hands is on the horse's crest; the weight of the lower body is in the heels; and the rider maintains a *three-point* contact, with the crotch in the saddle, the inner bones of the knees and the calves of the legs in light contact against the horse's sides.

3. The take-off. As the horse takes off, he throws the rider forward and upward. The hip angles close, the knee angles open, the ankle angles stay closed, the heels are driven down, carrying the rider's weight.

1. The rider is at a canter, riding with a three-point contact, the crotch deeply in the saddle, as he approaches the jump.

4. The flight. The rider holds his position.

5. The landing. The hip angles open, knee angles close, the rider starts to *sink* down—not *sit* down—in the saddle, the flexed-in ankles and inner bones of knees acting to absorb shock of landing.

INTERMEDIATE JUMPING

6. The rider resumes contact with the horse's mouth and continues the canter in the three-point contact.

Chapter V

ADVANCED JUMPING

By the time the rider is ready for advanced jumping, his hands should move up to the horse's crest automatically. The eyes should have formed the habit of looking up, focusing on some object within the line of vision. The heels should be down.

If, however, the rider finds his hands rotating backward, interfering with his horse's mouth, he should not hesitate to go back to the earlier jumping forms and practices. I have often thought that "pride goeth before a fall" must have been written expressly for those riders who are too proud to reach for the mane, or to get their hands up before a jump, but not too proud to come back on their horse's mouth in mid-air, ruin a horse's mouth and disposition, and finally, run the risk of falling off.

In riding, there is absolutely nothing to be gained and everything to be lost by attempting to try the higher fences before the rider's reactions are absolutely automatic at the lower fences.

The very great and very important difference between intermediate jumping and advanced jumping is that now the rider will be asked to jump out of hand.

Since the term, "jump out of hand," is so vastly misunderstood and misinterpreted, let me take a minute here to explain what jumping out of hand really means.

A rider may be said to be "jumping out of hand" when his security and balance in the saddle is such that he is able to maintain a direct line from the horse's mouth to the rider's elbow, before, during, and after the jump, with the same amount of pressure applied to the horse's mouth—never more nor less.

To illustrate to you how difficult this is: I had occasion, during the writing and illustrating of this book, to look for a picture of some rider negotiating a fence and jumping out of hand. Of a dozen or more top riders, young and old, including many who had won their Maclay cups in the National Horsemanship Event at Madison Square Garden, I couldn't find a single one who really jumped a horse out of hand, maintaining this straight line from horse's mouth to rider's elbow.

A broken line is not bad in itself if the rider's hands haven't dropped, thereby not only breaking the line from mouth to elbow, but, in dropping, bringing the bit against the bars of the horse's mouth and jabbing him almost as severely as though the rider had faulted in the other extreme and come back on his horse's mouth with his hands flying up into the air.

The line from mouth to elbow is maintained not because it looks good—which it does—but because while that line is maintained, the rider's body is necessarily in the correct position and the horse's mouth is not being interfered with in any way. That is why this line is the thing we strive for, and it is also why I prefer to have pupils use the mane, or press on the horse's crest, in the earlier stages when I know that attempting to jump out of hand will only result in a horse's being seriously interfered with or the rider sacrificing some of his security in the saddle.

Another important thing that comes into use here in this final stage of jumping is the rider's shock absorbers. His shock absorbers are his ankles and the inner bones of the knees. When the ankles are flexed in, and the heels are depressed, the shock of the horse's landing on the other side of the fence will be absorbed by the ankles, and by these inner bones of the knees which are kept in constant, light contact with the horse's sides. These shock absorbers are important in many ways: They reduce the shock of landing and so make it possible for the rider to maintain his position in the saddle when the horse lands. When the shock absorbers are not used, the rider's legs tend to shoot out in front of him. His body flies back, his hands go up in the air, and the whole position in the saddle is distorted.

That is why the rider should be able to keep his heels *down* before he attempts advanced jumping, which is jumping out of hand. If his shock absorbers are not working properly and he attempts to jump out of hand, he risks the loss of his security in the saddle and the almost certain knowledge that his horse is going to be interfered with either before, during, or after the jump.

The rider's position in the saddle, the smoothness with which his hands and upper body function, are all dependent on his security. Final and real security cannot be achieved until the heels are down and the rider's weight is actually carried in the heels. For that reason, the learner and the intermediate rider both are cautioned against trying to jump out of hand before this final security has been achieved, and the shock absorbers are able and ready to go to work for them.

But jumping out of hand is the goal toward which we are steadily and constantly working in everything we do, because jumping out of hand permits the maximum security and maximum control over the horse. It enables the rider to ride a course of jumps without wings with much less danger of run-outs than if the hands must be brought up three strides away from the fence. It means the rider can now attempt more difficult horses, because he is able to use all of his aids in controlling his horse. It is, of course, the *only* way to train or jump horses that refuse or run out.

But this ideal form of jumping is certainly something that anyone with the will and the patience to learn and learn properly can master. It is within the realm of any rider who will resist the temptation to hurry the early work or jump the bigger fences, before his reactions have become automatic, and before he finds his hands moving forward no matter what his horse does or what sudden emergency condition he encounters before a fence.

It is impossible for any rider to jump out of hand if the rider is either mentally or physically hanging back in the saddle. The rider must be confident, and he can be confident only if he has put in enough riding hours to build up his security in the saddle. And the longer the rider stays on cross-rails, the sooner he'll find himself able to jump his horse out of hand.

2. Moving into the approach, the rider assumes a three-point contact. Notice the line from horse's mouth to rider's elbow.

3. The take-off. The horse thrusts the rider forward, and upward but the line from horse's mouth to rider's elbow continues unbroken. *This is jumping out of hand, but should be attempted only after the seat is sufficiently secure to permit the hands to work independently of the body.*

1. The rider is in a galloping position, moving toward the jump with a two-point contact: Inner bones of the knees, calves of the legs in light contact against the sides of the horse. Heels down, eyes up.

4. The flight. Again, notice the line from mouth to elbow.

5. The landing, with the flexed-in ankles, the inner bones of the knees receiving the shock, enabling the rider to keep his position easily and maintain the unbroken line from mouth to elbow.

ADVANCED JUMPING

6. The rider sinks down in his saddle, and continues his contact with his horse's mouth.

THE CORRECT WAY TO RIDE A COURSE OF JUMPS

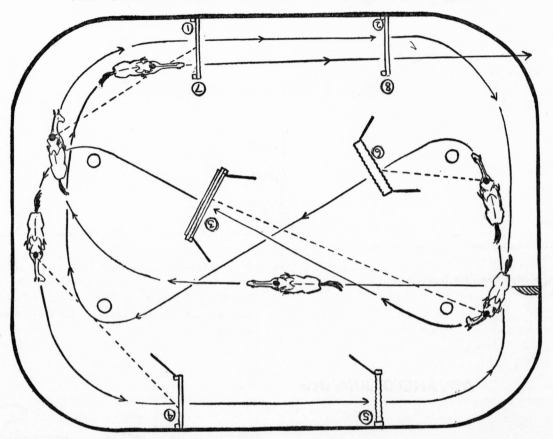

1. **Entering the ring.** The rider comes in at a walk, breaks into a slow trot, then a posting trot, and back to a slow trot, a canter, then a hard gallop.

2. He comes around the marker, his eyes on the jump ahead of him, riding a line of sight. If his horse attempts to cut into the jump, his *inside* leg becomes active to prevent it; if his horse's near side bulges out, the outside leg becomes active, bringing the horse together again.

3. Notice the line of sight while the rider uses the correct aids to make a smooth turn. His eyes are focused ahead of him, taking in everything within his range of vision, or line of sight.

4. Again, notice the line of sight as the rider concentrates on pace and eyes, while his aids, working automatically and with no conscious thought, turn his horse smoothly.

5. The rider's line of sight focuses on the jump ahead of him.

6. The rider looks straight ahead, finishes his course, brings his horse back to the trot, the slow trot, the walk. He relaxes tension on the reins as his horse relaxes, and *quietly* leaves the ring.

Chapter VI

RIDING A COURSE OF JUMPS

By the time the rider is ready to ride a course of jumps, he should be sufficiently advanced, and his reactions sufficiently automatic, so there is nothing on his mind but two things: getting and keeping his pace, and keeping his eyes focused in the direction of movement or on the next obstacle.

Remember: that the horse or rider is being judged from the minute he enters the ring until he leaves it. Bring your horse under control promptly and quietly after finishing a course of jumps.

The most important and crucial moment in the whole jump occurs *three strides away from the fence.* That is when the horse gives the rider the feeling of any disobedience he may be about to attempt, such as refusals or run-outs. That is when the rider, by being alert, prevents a run-out or a refusal.

When riding a course of jumps without wings, be careful of speed. The faster the horse goes, the faster he's apt to run out, and the more difficult for the rider to control.

Never add speed to correct a run-out. A run-out is punished and corrected by sudden, sharp pressure on the rein in the opposite direction from that in which the horse attempted to run out.

FOR THE BEGINNER OR THE RIDER WHO DOES NOT HAVE THE ADVANTAGE OF WORKING UNDER AN INSTRUCTOR: Run-outs, refusals and other problems can be reduced and sometimes eliminated entirely, if the rider will:

1. Settle his horse and, at the same time, establish the pace he wishes to take over the jumps by first galloping around the course, alongside the jumps. This gives the horse a chance to accustom himself to the terrain and any strange looking objects within his line of sight.

2. Take the jumps one at a time, and not in sequence. When a horse knows the way home, or the sequence of a course of jumps, he tends to increase his speed over the second half of the course. Therefore, it is sometimes wise to take the jumps individually and not in sequence, taking the horse up to the jump and showing it to him first if he tends to be a refuser.

3. If there is an in-and-out on the course, trouble can be avoided by taking down both the in *and* the out of one panel, on one side. When the horse has gone through smoothly once, raise the out and leave the in at the lower height. When this has been

successfully negotiated, both sides may be raised, and the chances are that the horse will go through smoothly.

4. Always avoid overschooling. More horses have been soured through overschooling than by any other single thing connected with horse showing. When your horse has put in a good, smooth performance with easy pace and a nice way of going, put him away and let it go at that.

It is always better to avoid trouble than to overcome it later on. For this reason, the rider who isn't quite sure of himself or his horse will do well to lower jumps where possible and smooth out the performance at the lower level before schooling over the jumps at their original height.

Chapter VII

HOW A WORKING HUNTER IS JUDGED

by

COLONEL WILLIAM H. HENDERSON

(Author's note: Colonel Henderson is as familiar to showgoers and show riders as ring and tanbark. A breeder of horses, a prominent horse show judge, a former member of the board of the American Horse Show Association, he speaks with a well-earned authority on the rules and methods used in judging working hunter classes at American horse shows.)

By far the most popular classes at horse shows today, with the exception of certain sections of the south, are the working hunter classes. This is so for two reasons: The breeding of the thoroughbred stock which produces most of our conformation hunters was so sharply curtailed as to have been at a virtual standstill during the war, and the effect of that curtailment is now being felt severely.

But the other, and better, reason for the increasing popularity of the working hunter divisions at the shows is a good one: It is because more and more people are learning to ride well enough to be able to compete in the show ring. It means that the horse show is returning to the amateur status, the country-fair feeling, where everyone who has anything at all to show wants to get in and ride his own horse and have fun doing it. That is what horse shows should be, and I like to see more and more owner-

riders and amateur riders coming along to make their debut in the show ring.

It is for those people, primarily, that this article was written, although there are some points in the judging of a working hunter class which sometimes rise up to confuse even the most seasoned show rider, and send him over to the judge for an explanation.

I shall try to answer most of those questions in this article.

To begin with, what *is* a working hunter?

A working hunter is any horse that is "hunting sound," and can jump a three-foot-six fence reasonably well and safely, in good jumping form. He need not have been hunted with a recognized pack of hounds, although this qualification is called for in some special classes, and the program clearly states this when it is so. The majority of working hunter classes do not require that a horse be "qualified," by having put in at least one season with a recognized pack of hounds.

To be a working hunter, your horse does not need to be of any special size or color, although sixteen hands is a good size because a sixteen-hand horse isn't so big that a rider who has to dismount for some reason in the field will have difficulty getting back in the saddle. A sixteen-hand horse, too, is generally built so that he looks as though he could carry the necessary amount of weight in the hunt field, and have enough stamina to enable him to stay with hounds, because although the working hunter need not have been hunted before appearing in the show ring, he is *always* judged on his suitability as a hunter.

The second thing you will want to know if you are fairly new at showing is, "How high will the fences be?"

The American Horse Show Association has broken horse shows down into three groups, or divisions, known as Class A shows, Class B, and Class C. The amount of money awarded, the number and variety of the classes, are the basis used for determining whether a show is a Class A, Class B, or Class C show.

At Class A shows, you may expect more than one four-foot fence. At Class B shows, you will probably find just the one four-foot fence which a show must have in a working hunter course in order to qualify as a recognized show. In Class C shows, you will probably find just the one four-foot fence, and the other jumps will, on the whole, be simpler and less formidable than the courses encountered at such Class A shows as Devon, Piping Rock, North Shore, and the National Horse Show at Madison Square Garden. If you are just beginning to show, the Class C shows—where the jumps are lower and the competition generally not quite so stiff— is the place to start.

I have used several terms familiar to all show riders, but probably not so familiar to the rider getting ready for his first show, and his first working hunter class. Just what *do* we mean by such terms as: Hunting sound, conformation faults not to count, ticks not to count unless the fault of bad jumping, etc.? I am going to explain the meanings of these familiar terms to you, and tell you what I will look for in your horse when, some-day, you ride him into a show ring where I am judging.

Because he *is* a Working Hunter, the first thing I am going to be looking for as you enter the ring and start on your course is, Manners. I am also going to be watching for manners as you exit from the ring. A working hunter who, finished with a course of jumps, can scarcely be held and goes plunging or lunging toward the outgate or the waiting van, is going to be marked down on manners, because I certainly wouldn't consider such a horse an agreeable mount to ride in the hunt field. And whether your working hunter ever has been hunted, or ever will be hunted, is beside the point. He is still judged according to how the judge thinks he would behave in the hunt field, and how pleasant a ride he would be to hounds.

Hunting Sound: Means exactly what it says, and like all working hunter judges, I adhere to both the spirit and the letter of that qualification. Again and again, I have had angry exhibitors come up to me to protest the award of a ribbon to a horse with a jack, or bone spavin; one with a deficiency in one eye, such as a "Feather," or a horse who, although he jogged out sound in one class, had jogged out lame in the class before.

What the horse did in the class before this one, or the show before this one, is not the concern of the judge and most judges try hard to forget the shows and the classes that preceded the one they are judging. A horse is "Hunting sound" if he jogs out sound at the end of the class in which he competed. He may go dead lame two seconds later, or been dead lame two seconds before. If he put in a good performance and jogged out sound at the finish of his class, he deserved the ribbon.

A horse is "Hunting sound" when he has no illness, blemish or conformation fault which would prevent his being able to jog out sound at the completion of his class. Conformation faults, as such, do not count against him, nor do honorable hunting scars, such as wire cuts, etc.

Windiness, obviously, will count against a horse and disqualify him, since a windy horse cannot stay with hounds or be safe when galloped for any length of time. But bone spavins, bog spavins, side-bones, and all the many other things which so often afflict the working hunter, do not count against him as long as they are not causing any immediate lameness or unsoundness. Your horse may enter the ring and have as good a chance as the best horse there, despite his bumps and blemishes, if they do not interfere with his performance over fences. That is what we mean by "Hunting sound."

Ticks not to count except when the fault of poor jumping is the next point on which your horse will be judged, and I shall have to fault him if he raps his fences because he got in wrong, stood back too far and "reached," or jumped without properly folding his front legs. Young horses and green horses, especially, tend to have this jumping fault, and it is one to watch out for in your own horse. When you study pictures which are sent to you from the show, you can generally tell by the way in which your horse is either folding or unfolding over the fence whether he is jumping without folding properly. If he is, it's not only bad for showing, but even dangerous, and some riding professional should be consulted as to the best way of breaking your horse of this habit and teaching it how to jump properly.

If a horse stands too far back and rubs a fence because of reaching, it means that he wouldn't be too safe over the unusual obstacles often found in the hunt field, and which have to be jumped on and off rough going. A horse that reaches for his fence is temporarily off balance, and might come down in a heap on the other side or, more often, turn himself over completely.

At the other extreme is the horse that gets in too close and rubs a fence because of poor judgment. Again, we count this tick as a jumping fault since it is a mark against his potential safety as a hunter.

I will *not* fault your horse if he has rubbed a fence simply because he jumps close and, therefore, safely. A hunter shouldn't jump like an open jumper. He should clear his fences but he should not "air" himself. On a long day's hunt, the horse who consistently jumps 'way over his fences will soon tire and go to the other extreme. The clever hunter is one who spares himself, who generally puts in a clean performance but who, because he measures his jumps so carefully, will sometimes rub one although jumping in good form.

So that is the answer to the question that I always hear running around the ringside at a horse show. "Do ticks count? The program says they don't, but the judge faulted my horse

because of just one light rap."

The judge faulted your horse because of one bad, risky, or dangerous jump, not because of the rap.

Pace: Is another important thing in a working hunter class. For the average working hunter, a pace of about sixteen to eighteen miles an hour is a good one. A somewhat faster pace for a longer course and higher jumps, a somewhat slower pace for a very short course with tricky turns and, usually, lower jumps. But above all, the best pace for your horse is the pace at which he jumps best and safest.

Remember, too, that once you have established a certain pace in a class on your first round, keep that pace rather than trying to slow it or to increase it. To change it tells the judge that your horse was either too rapid or too slow the first time, even though he jumped well and looked good. With the exception of a dangerously rapid pace, whatever pace you set over your first two fences should be the pace at which you continue. It should be fast enough to show the judge that your horse moves well enough to be able to keep up with the hunt even when hounds are running. But it must, of course, be completely controlled at all times.

Should the pace for a ladies' working hunter class be slower than the pace set for an open working hunter class? Not necessarily. The thing the judge looks for in any ladies-to-ride class is, outstandingly, good manners. Most horses look more controlled and jump with slightly less thrust when going a little more slowly. For this reason, the slower gait is sometimes preferred for this class. But a good, free-moving, easy-jumping horse is still what the judge is looking for, although in this class, as I say, the entire emphasis is on manners. It is highly desirable to ride a horse on a looser rein in this class, and his jumps should be smooth and consistent throughout. The horse who seems to require spurs, whip, or a strong hold on the reins does not, as a rule, impress the judge as a horse that would be an agreeable mount for a lady to ride to hounds.

Way of going: Means the way a horse moves, and is only

important in a working hunter class because a bad moving horse—by which I mean a horse who gallops high—is a horse that tends to tire easily on a long day's hunt and who usually gives his rider a fairly rough ride. A high-galloping horse is a high-trotting horse, and a high-trotting horse will wear out the hardiest rider toward the end of a five- or six-hour hunt. For this reason, the close mover, or "The daisy cutter," is what the judge thinks of as a good mover.

In all working hunter classes, Manners, Performance over fences, Substance, and, finally, Way of going, are scored on each horse. Therefore, when you set out to buy your first working hunter, be sure that he:

1. Responds fairly easily to legs and reins, as this is the basis of good manners in any horse.

2. Is "Hunting sound," having no faults or blemishes which will interfere with his performance over fences or his way of going.

3. Has good vision. A "Feather" is not important if it isn't such as to impair vision, but ophthalmia *is* important, and your horse's eyes should be carefully checked by the veterinarian.

4. Is a reasonably good mover, as much for your own comfort as for the ribbons he may win at the shows.

And last, but certainly not least, when you've bought your horse, learned to ride him well enough to feel you're ready for your first show, and made your entries, BE PREPARED TO ACCEPT THE JUDGE'S DECISION AS FINAL!

You'll have another chance at another show, but this is *this* judge's decision at *this* show, so take it with good grace and even better sportsmanship. If you have an honest doubt or any sincere question to ask, approach the judge in between classes, but don't go to him in any attitude of criticism or resentment.

And remember, too, that no matter what you know, or think you know, about the horse that's winning, it is well to bear in mind that someday *your* horse will be winning, so keep what you know—or think you know—to yourself. Many fine horses, like many fine people, have a past, and the sporting thing to do is—leave it there!

W. H. Henderson

PART IV

Chapter I

ADVANCED AIDS

Flexion and Collection

"Flexion" and "Collection" are rather overpowering terms that describe the effects produced by the action of reins and legs used to make a horse flex his poll or his jaw, helping to develop a good mouth and to put him on the bit, where he can be made to respond to the slightest command from the rider's legs.

Any horse can have at least a fair mouth. Most horses can have good mouths, if their owners and riders are willing to take the time and trouble to mouth them *before asking them to jump.* But even if the damage has already been done, some knowledge of the proper way to flex your horse, to collect him and to put him on the bit, can overcome much if not all of the damage of the early lack of training.

To a good saddle horse, of course, flexion and collection are essential. For a hunter, they are simply a means to the end of having a responsive, easily controlled horse.

The purpose of *flexion* is to teach the horse to flex his jaw and his poll and come back to the rider, instead of hanging in the rider's hands, boring, or fighting the pressure of the bit. All horses should be taught to flex, since it improves the horse's head carriage and makes him much more easily controlled.

There are two kinds of flexion: Direct flexion, and Lateral flexion. From the earlier chapters on the application and co-ordination of the aids, you know that by this I mean: Flexion that is produced directly, by the application of a *direct rein;* and flexion that is produced laterally by the application of an *indirect* rein.

In *all* of riding, the legs are used to produce impulsion, and the hands—via the rein aids—to regulate that impulsion. Therefore, in flexions, the hands collect and control; the legs impel; the hands again come into action to distribute that impulsion either directly or laterally.

And, too, as in all phases of riding, there is an easy way to teach a horse to flex, and a more complicated way. Even the comparative beginner can be taught the easy way to flex his horse. I think you will be rather surprised and very pleased with the result which even a few minutes of flexing your horse in a simple, elementary way will produce.

TO PRODUCE DIRECT FLEXION: First Stage:

1. This is teaching the horse to be on the bit, or to move up into the bit and take a normal feel of it with an extended neck. To do this, the rider takes a feel of his horse's mouth, the legs close against the horse's sides to force him to move up into the bit while the closed hands hold him there.

2. As soon as the horse has moved up into the bit and flexed, or relaxed his jaw, the rider relaxes his hands and legs instantly, thereby rewarding the horse for his obedience.

This is a fairly simple exercise, easily learned and quickly mastered. In the beginning, it is best to practice this exercise while standing still or walking.

DIRECT FLEXION: Second Stage:

Is slightly more complicated, is designed to teach the horse how to flex his jaw instead of merely relaxing it. This is done by:

1. Using a direct rein to take a feel of the horse's mouth, and then closing the legs against the horse's sides until he feels the horse's jaw relax. The instant the jaw relaxes—or "gives"— the rider decreases the tension on the reins and relaxes his legs, rewarding his horse for his obedience.

Direct Flexion. It works on a horse's jaw and poll directly.

2. If the rider is not sufficiently skilled to be able to *feel* the exact instant at which his horse has yielded, and flexed, then he should watch his horse's mouth. It is essential that the horse be rewarded *the instant* he has yielded, or this exercise will quickly boomerang and create a mouth problem instead of solving one.

This exercise is best practiced when asking the horse to decrease speed from a walk to a standstill.

DIRECT FLEXION: Third Stage:

1. After the horse has been taught to flex his jaw, he must be taught how to flex his poll. This is done with "Fixed hands," which are hands set to increase pressure on the horse's mouth, with the legs closed on the horse, and pressure not relaxed until the horse has yielded. The moment the horse flexes his poll, the fingers relax and the horse is thereby rewarded.

This exercise is more difficult than the two previous exercises which I have mentioned, because the rider takes a stronger hold, or feel of his horse's mouth, instead of merely establishing contact with the horse's mouth. Hands and legs both act strongly, and since the result, or effect, produced will be equally strong, it is not only necessary but imperative that the rider's aids be sufficiently well coordinated so that he feels the exact moment when his horse has yielded, and can yield pressure at the same time.

Again, it is suggested that this exercise be practiced when decreasing the horse's gait from a walk to a standstill.

Once both horse and rider have learned the different parts and stages of DIRECT FLEXION, the horse can be asked to execute the complete movement as a whole. This is done by:

1. Use of the Direct Rein aid. The fingers close on the reins to control forward motion while the legs act to produce impulsion until first the jaw and then the poll flexes.

2. The horse is simply put on the bit—as described above in Direct Flexion, First Stage—and the rider closes his legs against the horse's sides forcing him to flex first his jaw, and then his poll.

A horse learns more from DIRECT FLEXION than from merely being put on the bit. As you can see, in direct flexion, we have produced *collection,* whereas in the earliest and most elementary stage of flexion, the rider has simply made contact with his horse's mouth and held it, without the active use of his legs against the horse's sides.

Legs produce impulsion, hands control and distribute it. Therefore, when the direct rein aid is used strongly in conjunction with an active leg, we have collection. For a DIRECT FLEX-

ION the hands work to distribute that collection by forcing the horse to yield, or to flex.

DIRECT FLEXION makes it easy for a horse to displace weight from his forehand to his haunches. The same is true of collection at increased speeds. The faculty of being able to displace weight from forehand to haunches is invaluable in a hunter when making sharp turns at rapid speeds. A horse whose weight is on his haunches can make a sharp turn safely, whereas one whose weight is on his forehand may cross his front legs and go down.

LATERAL FLEXION: Differs from DIRECT FLEXION in that the jaw and poll yield on same side of the horse's head. This effect is obtained by the same methods as that used for DIRECT FLEXION, but instead of using the direct rein aid to accomplish flexion, the indirect rein is used, displacing the horse's weight laterally, or diagonally.

Lateral flexion is particularly useful for horses with extremely bad mouths. Such horses often put up strong resistance against direct flexion, but lateral flexion, in which, quite literally, first one side, then the other side, of a horse's mouth is flexed, will sometimes fool such an animal into yielding, and gradually improve his mouth.

Lateral Flexion. It works on one side of a horse's jaw and poll

COLLECTION

The first step toward collection is flexion, as I have described and outlined to you above. Once the horse has been put on the bit, and taught to flex his jaw and poll for longer periods at a time, he is said to be COLLECTED, and "In hand," or "On the hand," all riding terms which mean the same thing.

Because this is a book on horsemanship and not horsemastership, I haven't the time or the space to say as much as I would like to say to all riders—young and old, experienced and inexperienced—about the importance of taking time to put the horse on the bit, and to put him on it properly.

When a horse is behind the bit he is out of control. The purpose of putting a horse on the bit, through the proper use of the leg and rein aids, is to take that thousand or fifteen hundred pounds of horseflesh and put it up on the rider's hands where it may safely be controlled and directed. When a horse is behind the bit, the rider has the feeling of having "nothing in front of him." To compensate, the rider tends to get ahead of the horse, especially when jumping, but even when posting to the trot. The farther ahead the rider gets in this vicious circle, the farther behind the horse gets, and very often, when they reach the jump, they part company altogether, each going his different way.

Unless the horse is on the bit, or on the rider's hands, he can neither give nor receive signals. He can drop his head and quit at the last minute. He can run out. He can dog along at the walk or the trot, requiring the constant use of the rider's legs, spurs and voice to keep him going. He can be artificially put on the bit, for short periods at a time, with the use of these artificial aids. But in the long run, and in the long haul, the rider who has hurried his young horse into jumping before he has properly put him on the bit is in for many, many headaches, and many bad performances over fences.

WHEN YOUR HORSE IS ON THE BIT: He may be taught collection, but it should be done in very small doses, indeed, or the rider runs the risk of over-flexion and over-collection, which are very bad for a hunter. The horse's gaits become high and short, his neck is permanently over-arched, and his temperament, too, finally becomes affected by this continuous use of fixed hands and active legs. The combination will make all but the most placid horse excitable and over-anxious.

Collection, when it is done at all, should be practiced first at the walk, then at a trot, and finally at the canter.

The horse is first collected, as I have explained, by the strong use of the direct rein and the closed—or active—leg. He practices, first, the collected walk, which differs from the normal walk by a decrease in speed from approximately four miles an hour to three miles an hour, the higher action compensating for the loss of speed, as is true in all the collected gaits.

The same methods are used to obtain a collected trot and a collected canter, although it is a good idea to ask the horse to break into a collected slow canter from a collected slow trot.

A horse's normal trotting speed, as you know, is six to eight miles an hour, while his collected trot is closer to four or five miles an hour. His normal canter is ten to twelve miles an hour, while his collected canter is between six and eight miles an hour. The stride is shorter, the action higher and more animated.

The rider should not ask his horse to remain collected for long periods at a time. Be sure to reward him at frequent intervals by letting him extend his walk and travel with a floating rein.

All horses should be taught to flex, because it makes them easier to ride and to control. *Few* hunters should be asked for collection because it makes them higher-spirited, more anxious, and might, in time, affect the manner and the quality of their jump and their way of going.

THE FLYING CHANGES OF THE LEAD

When moving from a right lead to a left lead, the following aids are used to effect a flying change of the lead:

1. The horse is collected.

2. The left indirect rein is applied in front of the withers. At this time, the right rein is a direct rein, and a passive one.

3. The right leg becomes active, displacing the horse's haunches, forcing him to take the left lead.

The difference between the flying change of the lead and the ordinary change of the lead is, of course, the speed and smoothness with which the different aids must be applied, so that while each is applied separately, the effect is that of having been applied simultaneously. It is almost impossible, watching a skilled horseman make a flying change of the lead, to see the different aids being applied. For that reason, such high-school work should not be tried until the aids are working automatically with no conscious thought on the part of the rider as to their sequence.

LEARNING HOW TO MAKE THE FLYING CHANGE OF THE LEAD

From the canter on the right lead, decrease the gait to a trot, then apply the aids for a left lead. Repeat this exercise many times before asking the horse to make a flying change.

USE OF THE AIDS FOR THE EXTENDED TROT

When the horse is on the bit and doing a collected trot he can be taught to extend the trot. The rider's legs demand greater impulsion so that extension of hind legs drives the forehand to its greatest extension. As the horse extends, collection should be abandoned, light contact on horse's mouth for support, giving horse as much liberty of neck as possible.

THE USE OF THE AIDS FOR THE TWO-TRACK ILLUSTRATIONS

The horse is said to be two-tracking when he moves off the line of movement obliquely. The horse's head is turned in the direction of movement, the outside legs pass over and in front of the inside legs. The aids for the two track: Right leading rein, left leg active, displacing the haunches in the direction of movement. The left indirect rein in rear of the withers. The direction in which the horse moves at the two-track should not exceed forty-five degrees to his original position.

Chapter II

F. E. I. RULES
(*Federation Equestre International*)

Usually, when competing at an American horse show, you will be subjected to the rules of the American Horse Show Association. But more and more shows are putting in at least one class that is ridden under F. E. I. rules. Here is what they are and what they mean:

F. E. I. rules are the regulations laid down by the Federation Equestre International, the largest horse show governing body in the world.

What is the difference between F. E. I. rules and those of the American Horse Show Association, with which we are more familiar?

F. E. I. rules are very simple. An element of time is introduced along these lines: In the first round of each jumping class there is a time limit. Any horse going evenly and well will complete the course comfortably within this time limit. If he exceeds the time limit, he will be penalized ¼ fault for each second over the limit.

In addition he will be penalized: 4 faults for a knockdown, whether in front or behind, 3 faults for the first refusal, 6 faults for the second, and he will be eliminated for a third. In the case of a fall the rider may remount and continue the course; but time will run on throughout, and there will be a penalty of 8 faults.

A fall does *not* mean elimination as under A. H. S. A. rules. Ticks are not penalized in any way.

Jump-offs are judged on the basis of time and jumping faults, as follows:

Jumping faults are judged in the same way as in the first round.

Time is considered along these lines.

1. If two or more horses have clean rounds, the faster time wins.

2. If one horse has a clean round in slow time, and another horse makes a fault in faster time, the clean round wins.

3. If two horses have an equal number of faults, the one with faster time wins.

4. A horse with fewer faults in slow time beats a horse with more faults in faster time.

Jump-offs are held to determine all four places if necessary, though the time factor usually makes this unnecessary.

Why are classes, judged under F. E. I. rules, important for American horse shows? For this reason: as we all know and regret, the Army Horse Show Team, which has carried our flag into one set of Olympic Games after another, no longer exists. Future Olympic competition must depend on civilian effort. If we are to prepare a team for the next Olympic both horses and riders must be accustomed to the conditions under which they will be obliged to compete.

WHAT JUDGES ARE LOOKING FOR IN F. E. I. THREE-DAY EVENT SCHOOLING

At the halt.

The horse is in hand, standing squarely on four legs ready to obey the rider.

A free walk at 4 miles per hour.

The horse is extended and relaxed in hand. His steps should be equal and deliberate, and in cadence.

A collected walk at 3 miles per hour.

The horse is on the bit, flexed, and taking shorter steps.

An ordinary trot at 8 miles per hour.

This is a posting trot. The horse moves forward freely, with the left hind leg tracking the left fore in balance and relaxed. This is a two-beat gait.

An extended trot at 10 miles per hour.

This is also a posting trot with the horse extending behind producing extension in front without action.

A collected trot at 6 miles per hour.

This is a sitting trot. The horse is on the bit and flexed, taking shorter steps with compensating higher action.

An ordinary gallop at 10 to 12 miles per hour.

The horse is straight from head to tail, moving relaxed and in hand.

An extended gallop at 14 to 16 miles per hour.

The horse's head and neck are extended, the stride and pace increased, but the horse is still calm and relaxed.

A collected gallop at 8 to 10 miles per hour.

The haunches are active beneath the horse, the forehand is light and mobile.

HOW THE JUDGES WANT THESE MOVEMENTS EXECUTED

The change of pace and gaits should always be executed swiftly and promptly as they are called for.

The horse should be in hand and very light, responding easily as he is circled, or changes of direction are executed. There must be no abrupt movements.

When two-tracking, the head and neck should be going in the direction of movement.

Changes of lead in the air should be done in the period of suspension when the horse's four feet are off the ground.

The use of the voice, as in clucking, is forbidden.

Chapter III

FOX-HUNTING TRADITIONS

An Explanation Of What Is Required Of The
Horse And The Rider In The Hunt Field

by

HOMER GRAY, M.F.H.

Rombout Hounds
Poughkeepsie, New York

(*Author's Note: Mr. Gray is not only Master of Foxhounds of one of the finest and best organized hunts in the country; he is also in great demand as a judge of hunter events at leading horse shows everywhere in this country, including the National Horse Show at Madison Square Garden. Mr. Gray is a fine huntsman who is sincerely interested in seeing more and more people drawn to the thrilling and intensely rewarding sport of fox-hunting. The following article is for the guidance and instruction of those riders, both young and old, who are starting out on their first hunt.*)

The purpose of fox-hunting is to seek out, chase, and kill a fox with a pack of foxhounds. The purpose of fox-hunting is *not* to see how *many* jumps you can take in a day. If that is your desire, I would recommend you stay away from fox-hunting and take a good, long cross-country ride instead. But if you are going fox-hunting, then you are going out to combine two of the most thrilling sports in the world: galloping a good horse cross-country, and watching hounds work.

Too few people understand the importance of hounds and overestimate the importance of jumping on a hunt. As a result, a master is often irritated to the point of asking a noisy, talkative rider to turn his horse around and go home.

The hunt depends entirely on the skill with which the hounds work. You will have a good day's hunting or a bad day's hunting, a kill or draw a blank, depending on the hounds. Much of hunting tradition centers around the hounds, and even the rank beginner at hunting must know enough about it not to ruin a day's hunting for the rest of the field.

Therefore, in this short article, I am going to try to tell you what the different terms mean, why we observe these traditions, and how important they are.

The Hounds: It takes a good Huntsman years to learn how to work a pack of fox-hounds. The Hunt Club has begun by spending many thousands of dollars building up a good pack. It is up to the Huntsman to teach them obedience, and the Huntsman, in turn, must understand every sound they make, or every time they "speak." It is not important to the rider who has just begun to hunt to learn any of this, but it is not only important but also essential for him to realize what the Huntsman is trying to do. The hounds speak in many different tones and voices, which is referred to as "making music." It sounds like a cacophony of noise to the uninitiated. But even the slightest change of a hound's tone has told the Huntsman something about the fox he is seeking, and even the slightest noise from the field can throw him off.

For this reason, it is important that you hunt on a quiet, obedient horse. A restless horse, moving and stamping the ground, can drown out the sound of a far-off hound. *Talking is prohibited* during the check when the hounds are working. There will be other checks, when the hounds are re-cast, when it is permissible to talk, to move about, to have a stirrup-cup. But when hounds are working, the rule is—Silence, please!

The Meet: Is the term we use for the place where hounds and field will meet. Something called a "Fixture Card" is sent to all members of the hunt, and this tells you where the hunt will meet during the season. The place is changed as frequently as possible, of course, in order to keep hunting over new country. You will arrive *at least half an hour early,* so as to have time for any last-minute attentions to horse or self, and be certain of being in the saddle, ready to move off, at the appointed time.

If you are a new member, you will ride up to the Master, tip your hat, introduce yourself, and bid him good morning. At the end of the hunt, you will again ride up to him and thank him for a pleasant day's hunting.

The Master: Is, as a rule, someone who has lived in that country and hunted with that pack for many years. He is often the one who contributes large sums of money to keep the country paneled and guarantees landowners that they will be properly reimbursed for any damage to fields, fences, or crops. He is a man with a background of hunting tradition, and a person who loves all of its traditions sufficiently to work hard at the job of building up and keeping a good hunt. The Master is respected and deferred to at all times. Like the skipper on a ship, for as long as you are in the hunt field, his word is law.

The Huntsman: Handles the hounds, and is responsible for them. He may be either an amateur or a professional.

The Whips: Are exceptionally good riders, mounted on horses able to stay up with the Master and Huntsman. They, too, may be either amateurs, appointed by the Master, or professionals. They whip in any hounds that tend to stray or lag behind.

The Field: Is comprised of members of the hunt and their guests. Their position in the hunt field is based on seniority rights. The older members—older in point of membership, not age—stay up in front. New members stay behind. So, too, do all considerate riders who find themselves out on a horse they aren't sure they can control, or on a green horse which might be expected to refuse or run out. It is well to bear in mind that the hunt field is not the place to school a green horse. If you have one, keep him in back where he won't disturb or distress other riders.

Hunting Cries and Sounds to Know and Respond to: When the hounds start off from the meet to draw their first covert, the Huntsman blows his horn and this is the signal for the Field to start to move on. Later, when hounds begin to run and the Huntsman sees where they are headed, he sounds his horn again, and this means "Gone Away." The field follows, usually at a full gallop. Sometimes the field is crowded into a narrow road or a clump of woods, and the Huntsman, Master, Whips and other officers are on the far side of a jump, watching the hounds and waiting for their next move. Sometimes hounds or staff come back along the same path, at which time you will hear the cry of "Master, please," "Huntsman, please," or "Hound, please." When you do, *back* your horse off the road keeping your horse's *head,* not his hindquarters, toward the path along which the Master, Hounds, or Huntsman will be galloping.

Other sounds you will hear are "Ware hole," or "Ware wire," and as the signal comes to you, pass it along to the rider behind you promptly, as this is important.

If the Field has checked, and one of the members happens to see the fox breaking covert, he cries out, "View Halloa" or "Tally-ho," which indicates to the Master where the fox has broken or headed for.

Finally, *NEVER* take a jump until hounds have cleared it and are well out of the way.

These are the more familiar hunting cries, and the only ones the novice needs to know for his own and others' protection.

Hunt Colors: Are steeped in tradition, given charily, and

cherished by anyone lucky enough to have received that permission. Each season the Master grants permission for colors to be given to riders thought worthy of them. To earn your colors, it is usually necessary to have hunted anywhere from two to five years with a recognized hunt, coming out at least twice, and preferably three times a week.

Hunt colors are worn on the collars of ladies' black coats. The men wear their Hunt buttons, and receive the privilege of wearing pink coats and toppers. When you see anyone in the hunt field wearing a pink coat or hunt colors, you may be sure that here is someone who knows the country thoroughly and is a good person to follow.

Hunt Caps: Are worn only by junior members—under sixteen—, by the Master, Hunt servants, the Hunt staff, and ex-Masters. Everyone else wears a black derby or, with pinks, a topper.

Rat Catcher: Is the name given to the tweed riding coat which is worn in the cubbing season, before formal hunting begins, and also on week-days when black coats and white stocks are not called for. With a black coat, a white stock and a canary-yellow vest are also worn. A stock pin is a simple gold bar pin or gold safety pin and never anything fancy.

Capping Fee: Is the fee charged to the guest of a member and is a tradition begun in England, centuries ago, when hunts were not formal, or organized, and the hunt servant went about with his cap, collecting whatever anyone cared to contribute to the hunt. Now it is charged to help defray the expenses and cover damage done to fields or crops.

Hunting Seasons: Cubbing (so called because the young hounds are taken out to be worked and exercised) usually starts in August, after crops are out of the ground. Formal hunting, as a rule, begins sometime in October, when the weather is cool enough to permit horses to run for long hours without being exhausted from heat. The hunting season is extended for as long as possible, and if the winter is mild, hunting is sometimes continued right through February, until spring planting.

General Courtesy Hints: You will always be welcomed at a hunt if you remember that our traditions are something which we respect and like you to respect. Therefore:

Don't talk while hounds are working.

If you are a new member, stay to the rear.

If your horse refuses a fence, don't try to school him in the hunt field and risk having the whole field lose the hunt. Pull over to one side, and get in again at the end of the line.

Don't crowd coming down to fences. Out hunting, panels are often narrow, turns are sharp. Allow a horse's length between you and the horse ahead of you so that if a horse or rider goes down, there is no danger of your horse's stepping on him. Wait your turn at fences. Don't cut in on the horse ahead of you. Serious accidents can result.

Keep your eyes up. We hunt through dense woods sometimes, and come upon jumps unexpectedly. Look where you're going!

If a hunt servant is repairing or lowering a jump, *wait until he's finished. Don't try to keep up with the field. Wait and catch up later.*

Keep your distance, *but keep up!* By letting your horse drop back, you run the risk of not only losing the field yourself, but causing everyone behind you to do the same thing.

Don't take any more jumps than you have to. A horse gets enough work in a four- or five-hour hunt without being asked to take unnecessary jumps. The rest of the field is out to watch hounds work and, if possible, have a kill. If you want a cross-country ride take it by yourself.

If you can't hold your horse, GO HOME! There is nothing more dangerous in the hunt field than a horse out of control. He risks not only his rider's neck but also the necks of everyone else in the field. If your horse can't be held, turn him and take him home.

I think if you will abide by these few rules of courtesy which have been dictated by the tradition inherent in fox-hunting, you will be a pleasant person to have along on a hunt.

Homer B. Gray

Chapter IV

A WORD TO YOUNG RIDERS

by

MRS. CHARLES LEE HARPER

Chairman, Flat Saddle Equitation Committee (1950)
of the American Horse Show Association

(*Author's Note: Mrs. Harper is one of the most popular and most sought-after judges for junior equitation at horse shows throughout the country. Every young rider will be helped, I am sure, by this frank discussion of the problems of judging, and riding in, junior equitation events.*)

A young exhibitor, arriving at a horse show, usually remembers to bring all the necessary equipment, but often forgotten is the prime requisite—Sportsmanship.

This article is not intended for the many grand young sportsmen and sportswomen encountered in the show ring and hunting field. It is written for those who, often being new to the game and poorly advised, sometimes feel unfairly treated.

An important question that every young rider and his parents have asked themselves is—"Is it correct to ask the judge why you were placed down or out of the ribbons?" It is quite correct and often helpful, but there is a time and place and proper attitude.

The time to question a judge is after the class or when the judge is resting between classes.

Everyone admires good manners. A horse show judge is no exception. Simply introduce yourself, present your question, listen courteously to his answer, thank him and depart. A judge is pre-pared to explain his decision to an exhibitor provided the question is not an attempt to influence the judging. A judge will be pleased to answer your questions if he feels that you have an honest desire for self improvement. You may ask him on what point of your riding you have been faulted and perhaps receive information that will improve your performance in later classes. Neither you nor your parents should argue. Many judges have at some time been subjected to acts of discourtesy from a badly mannered child or an overly zealous parent. These arguments are embarrassing to a judge and certainly do nothing to enhance the future sportsmanship of the child. The judge has been invited to pass on your performance and render a decision. Although you may not agree, it was for this opinion that the Horse Show Committee issued their invitation. To approach a judge in anger with a feeling that you have been dealt with unfairly, while secretly hoping your resentment may influence future decisions, is extremely ill mannered.

The young exhibitor should bear in mind that he is being judged from the moment he enters the ring until the cards are signed. The rider is being judged on an over-all picture. This includes: appearance of both horse and rider, the rider's attitude towards his mount, the sympathy and adaptability of his hands, his demeanor towards the judges and the ring steward. He is also being judged on his alertness and intelligence in responding to any special request; and if the contestant does not comprehend what is required, he or she should request that the order be repeated.

It is unfair to both the rider and judge to attempt any requirement that has not been fully understood. Always respond promptly when you are summoned, execute your orders and line up quietly—laughing and talking among contestants is not only distracting but undesirable.

Every judge notes the young rider's behavior towards his mount. His method of correcting a disobedience—whether the punishment is administered calmly or with loss of temper to the extent of needless abuse to the horse's mouth and sides. Never inflict an unnecessary punishment, or one that the horse does not understand. You should expect and demand obedience, but remember it should be acquired by knowledge, kindness, and patience. A rider who cannot control his temper is generally one who cannot control his horse.

In horsemanship classes as in any other division of a horse show, neat, appropriate, well-cut clothes are a must. White stocks when worn should be scrupulously clean and fastened by a plain gold safety pin. For young ladies long hair is far more attractive when neatly secured in a net. If a derby is worn, a hat guard is in order. Many a performance has been spoiled by a horse startled by a derby rolling down his back. Hunting caps are permissible for children who have not reached their eighteenth birthday. Flowers belong to the Ladies' Harness Division and are out of place on a hunter.

The appearance of a well turned out horse, mane and tail neatly braided in solid colored thread—not gay rosettes—and all tack, well shined, soft and pliant, is a pleasure to see. The rider, too, must be immaculate, boots well polished and spurs, if worn, shined. Together they create an eye catching picture that is a a compliment to the judges, committee, and spectators.

The kindness, courage, and good sportsmanship that association with an equine friend imbues is brought to its zenith in horse show competition. It is here a youngster learns the graciousness of the winner and the smile of the loser. It rests with the young exhibitors to uphold the sporting traditions the generations before them so valiantly protected. They are the horsemen and horsewomen of the future. It is for this that today's judges enjoy working with them, for they feel they are sharing in molding the judges of tomorrow.

Mrs. Charles de Harper